W9-BVZ-717

Reforming Special Education

MIT Studies in American Politics and Public Policy
Martha Weinberg, general editor

Reforming Special Education:
Policy Implementation from State Level to Street Level

Richard A. Weatherley

The MIT Press
Cambridge, Massachusetts, and London, England

This book was set in Fototronic Zenith
by Dharma Press, and
printed and bound by The Alpine Press Inc.
in the United States of America

Library of Congress Cataloging in Publication Data

Weatherley, Richard.
  Reforming special education.

  (MIT studies in American politics and public policy; 5)
  Bibliography: p.
  Includes index.
  1. Handicapped children—Education—United States. I. Title. II. Series: Massachusetts Institute of Technology. MIT studies in American politics and public policy; 5.
LC4031.W4   371.9'0973   79-10715
ISBN 0-262-23094-1

To Florence and Bob,
Cathie and Peter

Contents

Series Foreword

Social scientists have increasingly directed their attention toward defining and understanding the field of public policy. Until recently public policy was considered to be a product of the actions of public institutions and as such was treated as the end point in analysis of the governmental process. But in recent years it has become clear that the public policymaking process is infinitely more complex than much of the literature of social science would imply. Government institutions do not act in isolation from each other, nor is their behavior independent of the substance of the policies with which they deal. Furthermore, arenas of public policy do not remain static; they respond to changes in their political, organizational, and technical environments. As a result, the process of making public policy can best be understood as one that involves a complicated interaction among government institutions, actors, and the particular characteristics of substantive policy areas.

The MIT Press series, *American Politics and Public Policy*, is made up of books that combine concerns for the substance of public policies with insights into the working of American political institutions. The series aims at broadening and enriching the literature on specific institutions and policy areas. But rather than focusing on either institutions or policies in isolation, the series features those studies that help describe and explain the environment in which policies are set. It includes books that examine policies at all stages of their development—formulation, execution, and implementation. In addition, the series features studies of public actors—executives, legislatures, courts, bureaucracies, professionals, and the media—that emphasize the political and organizational constraints under which they operate. Finally, the series includes books that treat public policy making as a process and help explain how policy unfolds over time.

Richard Weatherley's book, *Reforming Special Education*, analyzes the consequences of Chapter 766, the Massachusetts law designed to overhaul and improve provision of education for handicapped children. His study of the implementation of a policy designed to be a major reform proceeds from the assumption that laws designed to soften inequality may themselves become vehicles for perpetuating the biases of the political system. He focuses on the issue of how a major reform measure affects the behavior of front-line service workers, who have limited resources to do their jobs and who are charged with the task of providing better, fairer treatment to handicapped children. Weatherley asks a more subtle question than the traditional one of why programs fail in implementation. Instead, he asks how changes in policy affect the broader environment in which they are carried out and what the consequences are for thinking about the policymaking process.

Richard Weatherley teaches at the University of Washington.

Martha Wagner Weinberg

Foreword

The study of policy implementation focuses on the potential of democratic politics; it is based on the assumption that society is capable of constructing appropriate responses to changing needs. Policy implementation studies speak to questions of political leadership because they attempt to assess the relationship between executive, legislative, or administrative action and policy as it is ultimately experienced by the public.

Most studies of implementation assume that policymakers stand in a hierarchical relationship to those charged with carrying out the policy. The guiding question of such studies thus becomes how consistent are the actions of subordinates with the stated intentions of policymakers. Inconsistencies between the stated "rules" and actual behavior are treated as departures from command decisions or defects in systems of coordination.

Richard Weatherley's study of policy implementation takes a significantly different tack; it does not presume a capacity to command or coordinate. Rather, it focuses on policy implementation in which those who have to carry out policy generally have broad discretion to set priorities and establish work routines. Thus Weatherley departs from the usual assumptions about policy and its impact.

Chapter 766, the Massachusetts special education law that Weatherley studies, did not call for the construction of a facility, the distribution of funds, or the regulation of previously unrestricted activities. Rather, it added responsibilities to an already considerable set of obligations imposed on teachers and schools. When Dick Weatherley began this study, he was interested in how teachers and administrators would incorporate the new requirements into the already overwhelming responsibilities with which they were charged. Thus the central focus of this work is not whether the law was implemented but how the law was implemented and how it was neglected and what patterns may be discerned that govern the ways educators as a group accepted or rejected their new responsibilities.

The guiding assumption of this study, then, is that the patterns of individual responses to the requirements of the new law become, in effect, the policy of the state. If policymaking requires an effort to affect teacher behavior, the implementation of that policy consists of the aggregated responses of individual teachers in adjusting to new demands. The ambitious new special education law essentially requires educators to add activities and change their behavior and responses to children with special education needs. Dick Weatherley's great accomplishment in this book is to show in detail how teachers and administrators, striving in some way to accommodate the new requirements slanted implementation of the new law by incorporating its provisions in ways consistent with previous practices and processes.

The careful study of aggregated individual responses is not easily accomplished. It demands much more than reconstruction of executive decisions and analysis of budgetary indicators of program outcomes. Weatherley's work required detailed observation of teachers' responses to procedural requirements, tracking of the impact of teachers' actions on students presumably affected by the new law, and assessment of resource allocation among seven schools in three school systems. Only with such research was it possible to discover how teachers were responding to new demands, and what the implications of those responses were for students.

This study has already made its mark by significantly influencing the research that has been spawned in anticipation of the introduction of the new federal law requiring appropriate educational responses to handicapped children. But its influence should extend beyond the scope of special education, for it will also prove instructive in other policy areas where the law to be implemented requires change in the behavior of lower-level personnel. When one recognizes that many laws such as those affecting police, the courts, and health and social welfare policy often call for changes in the behavior of public employees, the potential significance of this model of implementation analysis becomes clear. Wherever such policy changes are called for, we may be guided by Dick Weatherley's approach to the relationship between the policy to be implemented and the response to new demands by those who are charged with carrying out that policy at the street level.

Michael Lipsky

Acknowledgments

This study was supported in part by the Russell Sage Foundation and the Bureau of Education for the Handicapped, Grant No. G00-75-0053. The findings and conclusions, however, are solely my responsibility.

Many people involved in special education affairs in Massachusetts assisted with the study. I am grateful to the many street-level bureaucrats and administrators who shared their concerns so openly. I especially wish to thank Milton Budoff and Cynthia Gilles for their early support and encouragement and Loren Dessonville and Lee Miringoff for their able assistance in the field research. Mitsi Vondrachek and Joan Hiltner are to be credited for their efficient preparation of the manuscript.

The formulation that most directly influenced this study is Michael Lipsky's observation that the work situations of public service personnel at the "street level" constrain policy implementation in predictable ways. (He elaborates this proposition in "Toward a Theory of Street-Level Bureaucracy," in Willis Hawley and Michael Lipsky, eds., *Theoretical Perspectives on Urban Politics* (Englewood Cliffs, N.J.: Prentice-Hall, 1976), pp. 186–212.) I also wish to thank Professor Lipsky for his continued interest and encouragement, as well as for his helpful suggestions throughout the study and during the preparation of the manuscript.

Before and during the course of the study Jeffrey Prottas, Carl Hosticka, and I had many stimulating discussions on the role of street-level bureaucracies. I am grateful for their ideas and support.

The late Jeffrey Pressman offered many valuable observations on the conceptualization of the research and implications of the findings. Cathie Martin, David Hawkins, Aaron Wildavsky, and Martin Rein provided a number of insightful comments on portions of the manuscript.

Charles Blaschke, president of Education Turnkey Systems, Maryann Hoff, Janet Simons, and Barbara Norton helped track down a number of recent reports and studies on special education reform efforts across the country. I have relied heavily on the excellent work of William H. Wilken, in collaboration with David O. Porter and John J. Callahan, to relate my findings to other recent developments in special education.

A portion of the material presented here has previously appeared in Richard Weatherley and Michael Lipsky, "Street-Level Bureaucrats and Institutional Innovation: Implementing Special Education Reform," *Harvard Educational Review* 47 (May 1977): 171–197.

Reforming Special Education

1
Introduction

In October 1975 Congress enacted what will probably be regarded as the most significant child welfare legislation of the 1970s, Public Law 94-142, the Education for All Handicapped Children Act. Its passage marked the culmination of efforts, through court action and state and federal legislation, to extend guarantees for a free and appropriate public education to all children, regardless of any handicap they might have. While the law offered financial incentives to states that agreed to carry out its provisions, the subsequent issuance of the regulations for Section 504 of the Rehabilitation Act of 1973 made these provisions mandatory.[1]

Unlike previous federal education initiatives, which provided funds to state and local education agencies with minimal or vague guidelines, PL 94-142 and the implementing regulations require specific activities. Terrell Bell, the U.S. commissioner of education at the time the law was passed, expressed a view shared by many critics concerned about federal encroachment on local education. He suggested that the law "went far beyond any other education measure in dictating the means, not just the ends, of education policy." Congress had become "a super school board."[2]

The law, at least potentially, represents a shift in the federal role in funding education. One observer suggests, "If PL 94-142 appropriations match authorizations, the federal government share of special education excess cost would rise from the current 14 percent to 40 percent [and] total 1982 appropriations under PL 94-142 would be over $3 billion, more than is currently spent on Title I of the Elementary and Secondary Education Act."[3] Few believe, however, that the full funding of the law will ever come about, and, in fact, funding for fiscal year (FY) 1979 and FY1980 is projected at well below the level authorized.

The law requires the states to guarantee a free and appropriate education for all handicapped children aged three through eighteen by September 1978 and aged three through twenty-one by September 1980.[4] (However, states are exempted from serving children under six and over seventeen years of age if this is inconsistent with state law.) States are required to undertake procedures to locate and identify all children needing special education and to develop for each child an individualized education program (IEP) that sets short-term and annual instructional goals along with the planning for educational and support services necessary to meet them. The IEP is to be developed jointly by a team composed of a representative of the school's special education department, the child's teacher, the child's parents, and other individuals appropriate to the child's handicap(s) "as necessary" at the discretion of the parents or school.

The IEP must be based not simply on one or two test scores, but on a broad assessment of the child's educational performance, academic and social functioning, prevocational, vocational, psychomotor, and self-help skills. Materials, instruments, and procedures used in these appraisals must be free of cultural bias.

✓ To correct the inappropriate segregation of handicapped children in special classes, the law requires that children needing special education be served in the least restrictive environment. The purpose is to assure that children are educated as far as possible in settings with nonhandicapped children, so that both may benefit from increased social interaction and so that handicapped youngsters may learn to adapt to settings for the nonhandicapped.

The assessment and planning procedures must be administered in a way that guarantees due process for children and parents. Parents are to be involved in the development of the educational plans, notified of procedures to be followed in assessment and placement, and afforded impartial due-process hearings if they disagree with provisions of the educational plan.

Entitlements are based on a formula providing a maximum grant per year equal to the number of handicapped children in the state receiving special education services, multiplied by a percentage of the national average per-pupil expenditure ($1430 in FY1976). This percentage of the national average per-pupil expenditure increases over a five-year period. The multiplier authorized was 5 percent for FY1978, 10 percent for FY1979, 20 percent for FY1980, 30 percent for FY1981, and 40 percent for FY1982 and each year thereafter. Funds are to be passed to local education agencies with no more than 25 percent retained by state education agencies. The state may use 5 percent of its share or $200,000, whichever is greater, for administrative costs, but the balance must be used for direct and support services.

Early efforts to implement PL 94–142 have already stirred controversy over a number of policy issues that are likely to be debated for some time to come. While many agree with its objectives, there is considerably less consensus over the feasibility of attaining them through the remedies prescribed by the law. Federal social legislation has frequently fallen short of achieving intended goals because of insufficient funding, lack of enforcement, the absence of a bureaucratic infrastructure capable of facilitating implementation, or in some instances because the problems addressed were not amenable to solution through the interventions provided.

Some have contrasted implementation of PL 94–142 with Title I of the Elementary and Secondary Education Act. The latter provided federal funds to state and localities with few restrictions, while PL 94–142 offers many restrictions and few funds, at least initially. (The first year's allocations were about $70 per handicapped child. The national average excess cost, the amount beyond the usual cost of educating a nonhandicapped child, has been estimated at about $1200 per pupil.)[5]

Will the requirements of PL 94–142 bring about widespread adoption of uniform practices for equitable treatment of handicapped children? Or will they just create more work for school personnel? Will the guarantee of a free and appropriate education with necessary support services for the handicapped be realized? Or will the law simply "accelerate the trend toward senseless federal disruption of the governance and administration of our public schools," as one critic has predicted?[6] What happens to a universalistic policy—in this instance a policy for all handicapped children—when it is superimposed on a social order characterized by substantial disparities in local resources and individual wealth and power? What specific factors impede or facilitate the implementation of PL 94–142? Under what conditions can a public service bureaucracy charged with processing children on a mass basis effectively assess and serve individuals? Will the programmatic emphasis and allocation of resources for the education of the handicapped create a backlash of resentment from parents and educators in the regular education sector?

Definitive answers to these and related policy questions await further experience with the law. Before its passage, however, a number of states had already enacted special education legislation incorporating to a greater or lesser degree provisions subsequently incorporated in PL 94–142.

This study examines the experience of one such state, Massachusetts, in implementing special education reform. The Massachusetts Comprehensive Special Education Law, Chapter 766, passed in 1972, became effective in September 1974. It is rightly regarded as landmark legislation. In some respects it goes even further than federal law, embracing, as one writer observed, "almost the entire reform agenda of most child advocacy groups."[7] Federal officials cite Massachusetts as an exemplar of special education reform. The chairman of the Federal Bureau of Education for the Handicapped Administrative Review Team reported that Massachusetts had "located, identified, evaluated, and placed 99.9 percent of the handicapped population [and was] 99 percent in compliance with the federal law," placing it far ahead of other states.[8] (Either this appraisal was overly optimistic, or the compliance of other states was particularly abysmal.)

On a purely descriptive level, this study of the implementation of Massachusetts' Chapter 766 illustrates the substantial benefits to children resulting from special education reform; however, it also shows the kinds of problems and constraints encountered in attempting to mount a major reform that requires changes in the work habits of personnel in a public service bureaucracy.

This study focuses on the important role of front-line personnel in determining the nature and distribution of benefits to the public. It shows how these personnel, through their informal adjustments to the work environment, distort the policies they are charged with implementing and, in doing so, become policymakers in their own right. At the same time, it examines the implications of these collective job-coping adjustments for clients. It shows how the need to conserve limited resources results in priorities that benefit the more affluent and penalize the poor. These findings question the sufficiency of reform efforts that seek to improve the status of disadvantaged groups by attempting to alter the practices of public bureaucracies.

In recent years social scientists have increasingly focused on the process of policy implementation. This development has its origins in an increased concern with the distribution of public benefits,[9] recognition that the official formulation of government policy may indicate little about what governments actually do,[10] and an interest in explaining the apparent failures of many of the social welfare initiatives of the 1960s. Many studies have examined the activities of public officials in the legislative arena and in key policymaking and administrative roles at the federal, state, and local levels.[11] Explanations of policy failures have tended to focus on problems of coordination, on vague and conflicting priorities, and on objectives among and between governmental units in the policy "chain."[12] It is hardly surprising that these studies conclude that federal policy often "fails" because some governmental units in the highly decentralized, multiple-decision-point American political system are sufficiently powerful to veto or effectively undermine the original policy.

While it does not neglect the implementation constraints and barriers attributable to interorganizational, administrative, and leadership deficits, this study concentrates on a relatively unexamined limitation to implementation activities. It focuses on the ways in which the work situations of lower-level personnel in a public service bureaucracy limit and alter the implementation of reform objectives. While this study concerns implementation of a statute affecting educational personnel, the findings have implications for governmental efforts to change the work requirements not only of teachers but also of the police, welfare workers, legal assistance lawyers, lower-court judges, health workers, and other public employees who interact with the public and whose decision making calls for both individual initiatives and considerable routinization.

Public employees who work in such jobs share similar work situations. They have been called "street-level bureaucrats" because they occupy front-line positions and interact directly with citizens in the course of their jobs.[13] Typically, personal and organizational resources are severely limited in relation to the tasks they are asked to perform, and the demand for their services is always as great as their ability to supply services, unless services are rationed or otherwise limited.[14] To accomplish their required tasks, street-level bureaucrats must find ways of accommodating the demands on them and confronting the reality of personal and organizational limitations. They do this by routinizing, modifying goals, rationing their services, redefining or limiting the clientele to be served, controlling clients, asserting priorities, and generally developing practices that permit them to process the work they are required to do *in some way.* Caught between the limitations of their work settings, the demands of their clients, and the formal expectations of their work roles they characteristically experience considerable stress in the performance of their duties. This stress may be manifested by a high incidence of "burnout," a retreat into work rituals, and cynicism toward both superiors and clients alike.[15]

Street-level bureaucrats share additional work characteristics of some significance. Their work is inherently discretionary. There are limits to the extent the society can dictate standards for performance practices. Their professional or semiprofessional status ensures a measure of freedom from the expectations of the larger society.[16] Moreover the vague and competing objectives of the public services, the difficulty of establishing or imposing valid work performance measures, and the insignificance of the clients as a reference group mean that within certain professional and cultural limits some of the influences on their behavior that might otherwise be forthcoming do not in fact dictate behavior very much. Street-level bureaucrats are constrained by official policies and regulations, yet they remain relatively free to develop mechanisms for coping with their jobs.

These work accommodations are not random or idiosyncratic; they form patterns of behavior that in effect become the government benefits or sanctions "delivered" to the public. The structural conditions that provide considerable latitude or discretion in defining the way tasks are performed mean that street-level bureaucrats *are* the policymakers in their work arenas.[17]

Although they do not view their efforts this way, those who formulate new laws and policies attempt to alter the roles of street-level bureaucrats and hence the service they deliver. They can only hope to influence the work-role definitions that street-level bureaucrats "make" for themselves. Thus the study of implementation of policy formulated at the federal or state level for street-level bureaucrats requires a twin focus. On the one hand, one must trace the fate of the policy in traditional fashion (if it may be called that) from its authoritative articulation through various administrative modifications and alterations in order to discover the ways in which this "policy" affects the context of street-level decision making. At the same time, one must study street-level bureaucrats within their work context to discover how their ongoing decision making about clients is modified, if at all, by the new policy. This second approach turns the usual study of implementation on its head, for the lowest levels of the policy "chain" are now regarded as the "makers" of policy, and the "higher" level of decision making as circumscribing (albeit in important ways) the lower-level policymaking context.[18]

In the conventional view of implementation, illustrated in figure 1, policy emanates from the top and is carried out through successively lower organizational levels. This view conceptually imposes an artificial degree of order on an inherently disorderly process. This study suggests that policymaking takes place at the so-called delivery level as well (shown as broken lines in figure 1) and in turn may have some impact on actions of official policymakers and administrators at all levels of the implementation chain.

In this study of Chapter 766 I examine the policy implementation activities at the top, tracing the development and enactment of the law and considering how the state educational bureaucracy prepared to carry it out. Yet this analysis treats these actions at the state level as contextual background to policy implementation and policymaking functions at the street level.

There are inherent limitations to policies that seek to provide equal access to public benefits in a social and political order biased against the poor and powerless. Anthony Downs has observed that public bureaucracies provide a mechanism for assuring that private motives will lead officials to carry out public interests. He goes on to say, however, "It is our ironic conclusion that bureaucracies have few places for officials who are loyal to society as a whole."[19]

In the case of special education reform, the goal of educating *all* handicapped children is being carried out in a way that serves some

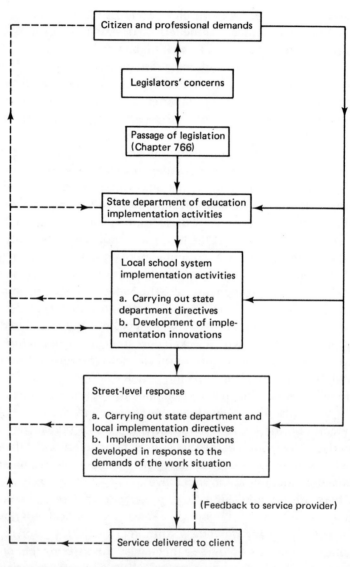

Note: The broken lines represent new demands, based on what is actually occurring at the local school system and service delivery levels.

Figure 1
Chapter 766: The Policy Implementation Chain

children better than others and some not at all. This is occurring despite a strong federal law that, as one analyst noted, represents "a quantum jump increase in federal regulation" of activities of education agencies at the state and local levels.[20] Paradoxically, the distortions in meeting these goals are not due to intentional evasions of the law or to actions of prejudiced, inept, or evil officials. To the contrary, the sincere and even zealous efforts of public officials to implement these policies result in a systematic distortion in their application. At the organizational level great disparities may be found among individual states, school districts, and schools in the identification and classification of handicapped children and in the scope and quality of services available to them.[21] These disparities are directly associated with the relative wealth of states and communities. As one study comparing special education expenditures concluded:

Wealth can exercise more control over the quality of local special education services in some states than all other influences combined. The richer the local school system, the more it is likely to do for handicapped children. . . . Local expenditures in Massachusetts rise in lockstep with its level of local income. Children from affluent families are likely to be served relatively well; children from poor families are likely to go begging. Private wealth determines public education.[22]

The Massachusetts special education law has an equalizing formula specifically designed to distribute state funds so that poor districts fare relatively better than the rich. Yet the wealthier districts have the staff resources and sophistication to get more from the state, both absolutely and relatively, than poorer districts,[23] and the disparities between rich and poor communities are actually widening.[24] An internal Massachusetts Department of Education report concludes:

There appear to be two disturbingly regressive relationships with respect to equalization. Communities with higher than average family income tended to receive more aid per child [from the state] and communities with concentrations of minorities tended to receive less than the average state aid dollars per child for special education.[25]

Wealthier districts also do better in securing additional federal discretionary grants to supplement their special education programs.[26]

Nationally, funding and service disparities are also likely to be aggravated by PL 94–142. Local entitlements are based on the number of children served in special education programs and, in general, since wealthier districts serve more children, they get more money.[27]

Collectively and individually, the affluent are better able than the poor to make public bureaucracies work for them. Wilken and Callahan, in their study of disparities in special education across the country, found parent pressure to be an important determinant of local services. Such pressure, they suggest, "keeps the needs of handicapped children in the mind's eye of local officials" and gives such officials an excuse to make improvements that are costly or politically unpopular. However, they also found that "well-organized and widespread parent pressure tends to be concentrated much more in some communities than in others," and "almost always seems greatest in middle-class suburbs of high-income professionals."[28]

This study, too, demonstrates the power of organized parent and advocacy groups. These groups are predominantly composed of middle-class professionals, and their local memberships are concentrated in the more affluent suburban communities. In Massachusetts affluent parents are more successful in placing their children, at public expense, in the more costly private residential and day schools.[29] A special commission of the Massachusetts legislature studying Chapter 766 concluded that "the parents who have greater access and knowledge of the system may receive more services for their children, perhaps reducing aid for some children who have greater needs."[30] Middle-class parents are better able to find out what services are available and hold the responsible agencies accountable for providing these services. The fragmentation of human service delivery, restrictive means tests for eligibility, and the relative difficulty in obtaining their services can lead to a dual system of services, one for the children of the poor and another for children of the affluent.

Due-process and appeal procedures are used to advantage by the more well-to-do and almost not at all by the poor. School officials are more deferential and more inclined to extend services to children of professional and relatively affluent parents. Others have noted that nearly all appeals under Chapter 766 have come from ✓ affluent Boston suburbs and few from Boston itself, despite its record of discriminatory practices in special education.[31]

It would be incorrect to assume that if the poor are served poorly, all others are served well. The street-level bureaucrats of this study, teachers and educational specialists, while striving to carry out impossible requirements given chronically insufficient resources, invoked solutions that tended to undermine the individualizing thrust of the law, reduced the mandated role of parents, restricted services, and frustrated attempts to bring handicapped children into the educational mainstream. This occurred in wealthy districts as well as in poor ones, and it happened even as these same officials were trying, frequently at great personal cost, to carry out policy objectives they supported.

The losers are not just the children and parents who are denied public services guaranteed by law, although they may be the ones who suffer the most. The street-level bureaucrats are themselves victimized by laws requiring work that, because of insufficient resources, they cannot hope to accomplish. They find themselves ✓ caught between demands from parents for services and from administrators to conserve resources. Regular and special class teachers and educational specialists become pitted against one another in struggles over status and over control of resources and of the work environment. Together they may battle their counterparts in other underfunded public bureaucracies, each seeking to shift responsibility elsewhere in order to save money. They suffer guilt at their inability to serve their clientele properly and are often blamed collectively for the failure of their organizations to accomplish mandated objectives.

The cornerstone of the new special education policy is the Individual Education Plan (IEP), which is based on a team assessment of each child's strengths, abilities, deficits, and learning potential as shown through several different kinds of assessment mechanism. It is here that the ideal of careful team deliberation with the collaboration of teachers, parents, and educational specialists confronts the reality of too many assessments to be done, too few people to do them, too few services to offer. Like street-level bureaucrats in hospitals, welfare offices, courts, police precincts, or mental health centers, school personnel cope as best they can, seeking ways to set priorities and routinize procedures and to restrict service options to limit the time, money, personnel, and resources required. These informal coping mechanisms are usually invoked in an effort to do the job as well as possible under existing circumstances, not with any intent to deny clients the benefits and procedural protections guaranteed by law. Yet the result of these actions taken by individuals seeking to manage unmanageable demands is to subvert the distribution of legally guaranteed benefits.

Two additional problems with team assessments should be noted. The IEPs are based on what may be termed a medical, clinical, or individual deficit model. The focus is primarily on the child and the interventions that might be applied to ameliorate the child's functioning. Too often this leads to a preoccupation with the child's supposed deficits and a neglect of environmental factors—the home and family situation and most importantly the school itself—that may be part of the problem.[32] Solutions are most likely to be directed toward changing the child and fitting him or her into the existing educational framework, ignoring the facets of the school, home, and community that constrain the child's learning and growth. The medical model can also foster an atmosphere of "blaming the victim," in this instance the children, their parents, and on occasion the classroom teachers, who are the least powerful members of the planning teams.[33]

This drawback leads to a second difficulty, also generally unrecognized and rarely acknowledged by school personnel. The medical assessment paradigm suggests an orderly rational decision process in which diagnostic evidence is weighed and service options decided jointly by participating team members based on this evidence. My observations of these deliberations show contrasting paradigms operating at the same time, again generally unacknowledged by participants. Team educational planning meetings may alternatively be viewed as a political bargaining process with participants of unequal rank vying with one another over issues of status, power, control, command of limited programmatic resources, and distribution of public benefits to clients. Political tactics of coalition building and caucusing, lobbying, logrolling, oratory, and the selective mobilization of information are all practiced, although not openly acknowledged, in these team deliberations. None of the participants' professional training prepares them for such intrabureaucratic political struggles. Some actors do better than others, and this difference has profound implications for all participants, most importantly for the children whose fate is being decided.

The use of a medical model to cloak a political process is not unique to school settings. Bureaucracies are based upon technical and functional specialization, and human service bureaucracies characteristically employ multidisciplinary staff in front-line positions. Many apply, at least implicitly, a medical model to diagnose and treat clients. While this may be obvious in the case of hospitals and other health and mental health settings, it is equally true of other kinds of human service including public assistance and social service, employment, lower court, and probation and parole agencies. The kinds of survival strategy and job-coping mechanism observed in this study may also be found in many other street-level bureaucracies and may similarly distort the distribution of their services. What this means for reform policies directed toward changing the nature of bureaucratic interventions is discussed in the concluding chapter.

Methodology

During the first year of implementation of the Massachusetts special education reform law, September 1974 through June 1975, I conducted extensive interviews of school personnel at the state and local levels, as well as with others who played key roles in the passage of Chapter 766, the development of administrative regulations, and their implementation. I sought to observe the responses of local school personnel to increased and altered work requirements as these responses were occurring. I selected three school systems and seven schools within these systems for more intensive study. In addition to analyzing the records of all children processed under the provisions of the new law by the three school systems, I observed meetings where educational plans for individual children were developed and traced the implementation of educational plans through interviews with classroom teachers. I also observed administrative meetings and conferences of special education personnel in the three systems and attended a number of statewide meetings of state and local special education staff throughout the school year.

The Massachusetts law has attracted considerable attention both within and outside the state and has been the subject of study by other researchers. I have tried to supplement my findings wherever possible with more recent reports of developments in Massachusetts and elsewhere as states now struggle to comply with the provisions of PL 94-142.

I
STATE-LEVEL POLICY

2
From Reform Concept to Legislation:
The Enactment of Chapter 766

The impetus for special education reform in Massachusetts, in other states, and ultimately at the federal level may be traced to several related developments.[1] First, special education scholars have increasingly questioned the efficacy of special classes and have advocated a more generic and less segregated approach. While the issue is still being debated, available evidence suggests that children in special classes do not necessarily learn better.[2] One early critic of overreliance on special classes stated:

It is indeed paradoxical that mentally handicapped children having teachers especially trained, having more money (per capita) spent on their education, and being enrolled in classes with fewer children and a program designed to provide for their unique needs, should be accomplishing the objectives of their education at the same or lower level than similar mentally handicapped children who have not had these advantages and have been forced to remain in the regular grades.[3]

Second, the process by which children were evaluated, classified, and assigned to special classes came under attack as being unduly arbitrary, culturally biased, and often motivated more by the desire to get rid of troublesome youngsters than to educate them. For example, a 1970 survey of special education programs in the Boston schools revealed the lack of a uniform policy; failure to provide assessments and services required by state law; widespread misclassification of children of normal intelligence as retarded; use of special classes as dumping grounds, sometimes by rigging results of Stanford-Binet tests to justify exclusion of troublesome youngsters from regular classes; and denial of special services for those in need of them. "Black children make up less than 20 percent of the total public school population," the report noted, "yet more than half the children placed in special classes for the emotionally disturbed are Black. None of the classes are in the Black community." The role of special education was summarized in the report:

"Special services" in the Boston School Department, then serve the system rather than the children. They are utilized to relieve the regular system of its responsibility toward certain groups of children. Administrators and teachers in the "special services" . . . are forced to become "babysitters" for the children that the regular system does not want.[4]

A third factor was probably the growing recognition that institutionalization of handicapped children sometimes amounted to little more than warehousing and that for some children more humane and efficacious community-based alternatives could be developed. The state's Chapter 750 legislation passed in 1962 provided up to $7500 per child for private placement of children labeled moderately or severely disturbed; but comparable support for the development of local service alternatives was not available. The law, by providing financial incentives, actually encouraged institutionalization and probably impeded the development of local community-based programs.[5]

In Massachusetts deinstitutionalization of handicapped children also gained impetus through the barrage of publicity accompanying the precipitous closing of correctional institutions for youthful offenders by Jerome Miller, the state's director of the Division of Youth Services.[6]

A fourth concern has been the categorization and labeling of children to facilitate their processing by schools. Labels such as "emotionally disturbed," "retarded," "learning disabled," or "brain-damaged" call attention to a single presumed deficit of a child to the neglect of the full range of characteristics that might describe that child's capabilities. This medical-pathological terminology stresses the child's alleged deviance from the norm rather than his or her developmental potential.[7]

Although definitions of these categories remain imprecise, changing from time to time and from place to place, assessment has too frequently meant the assignment of a label that is then taken as an explanation of the child's learning problem and a prescription for a specific mode of intervention.[8] The recent history of the category "learning disabled" illustrates the problem. In 1973 only 7.5 percent of all special education students were categorized as learning disabled; by 1976 this had increased to 18 percent, making learning disabilities second only to speech impairment as the most common disability. The reported incidence varied in 1976 from a high of 30 percent in the West to a low of 11.5 percent in the Midwest.[9] Professionals disagree on the meaning of the term, and some even doubt that it is a widespread phenomenon. Yet it is a more desirable and less stigmatizing category than mentally retarded. It may come as no great surprise that "Black children are classified in disproportionately high numbers as mentally retarded, while learning disabilities seem to be an affliction of White suburban children."[10]

Labels persist and serve to stigmatize the child as deviant or deficient; teachers have lower expectations of labeled than non-labeled children.[11] Programs designed in response to such unidimensional labels are frequently themselves unidimensional, reflecting in part the categorical approach to special education training whereby teachers have specialized in working with emotionally disturbed, retarded, or physically handicapped children, for example.[12]

A further consequence of the categorical approach has been the accretion of unrelated and frequently conflicting laws, programs, and school reimbursement formulas for categories of children. This legal state reflects a history of legislative response to the lobbying efforts of parents organized in categorical interest groups, often supported by special educators trained in categorical specialties. The result was the favoring of certain groups to the neglect of those who did not fit into a recognized category. Massachusetts statutes before the passage of Chapter 766 provided for differing education services for aphasic, deaf, speech-handicapped, hearing-impaired, blind, visually handicapped, mentally retarded, physically handicapped, emotionally disturbed, and perceptually handicapped children. Statutes also provided for noneducational services for such groups as "epileptics," "crippled and deformed children," "persons suffering from extrapulmonary tuberculosis, persons crippled by polio-myelitis, arthritis or muscular dystrophy, . . . children born with congenital deformities or birth injuries," and "children deprived of normal physical, mental, spiritual and moral development because of family problems."[13]

The Passage of Chapter 766, the Massachusetts Comprehensive Special Education Law

The preparation and publication of a critical evaluation of the state's education program for retarded children in 1970, closely followed by equally critical assessments of special education by the Task Force for Children Out of School, and by the Massachusetts Advisory Council on Education, provided a clear mandate for change.[14] Taken together, these studies portrayed a situation in which handicapped children were often overlooked or excluded from school and capriciously evaluated, labeled, and mislabeled. They were frequently shunted into special classes and denied services available to children in regular programs. While these studies noted examples of exemplary programs, the overall picture was one of ill-conceived, poorly administered, and underfinanced programs.

Exposure of injustice is in itself rarely sufficient to bring about its redress, as abundant evidence may attest. Furthermore, parent groups, which perhaps had the most to gain from reform of special education programs as well as some power to influence legislation, were under some constraints to seek only incremental improvements in existing legislation.

Both a cause and an effect of the categorical approach, nationally as well as in Massachusetts, was the competition among parent groups for statutory recognition and for a share of the limited resources for children afflicted with a particular handicap. This competition stood in the way of reform. Each group had reason to fear, based on past experience, that gains they had won might be lost and that other groups might fare better were they to back away from their insistence on explicit recognition for their group's interests. The public services that were currently available for specific categories of handicapped children had been won, after all, through the concerted pressure of groups organized around specific categories.

Despite these constraints, a particular confluence of circumstances favored passage of special education reform legislation in Massachusetts in 1972. Among these circumstances were a well-informed nucleus of reform advocates, skilled legislative committee research staff, influential legislative sponsors, and legislators pressured by constituent complaints of inadequate programs and motivated by their own concerns over burgeoning costs. In the background loomed the possibility of court-imposed reform.

Under the leadership of House Speaker David Bartley, the Massachusetts legislature had recently increased the staff research positions assigned to the Joint Committee on Education. Representative Michael Daly, chairman of that committee, had previously served as a member of the Task Force for Children Out of School, the group responsible for an influential report criticizing special education practices in Massachusetts. In 1971 he and Speaker Bartley, both former Boston school teachers, successfully cosponsored another reform effort, the Bilingual Education Act. Following that effort, Daly put his committee staff to work researching and drafting special education reform legislation. Much of the work had already been done. The 1971 MACE report included an analysis of existing state special education statutes and a model reform statute.[15]

Daly's decision to introduce special education reform legislation was also based in part on his reading of constituent interest. One index of such interest was the more than one hundred special education bills that had been introduced in 1971; many of these addressed the plight of parents seeking state-financed private school placements for their children.[16] While Chapter 750 provided that parents could place their emotionally disturbed children in private institutions at state expense, the limited number of openings resulted in long waiting lists and complaints to members of the legislature. Legislators were also concerned about the high costs of institutional care. The Chapter 750 program, passed in 1962 with an allocation of $1 million, cost more than $10 million by 1969 without coming close to meeting the demand.[17]

In October 1971 the nucleus for what later became the Coalition For Special Education was convened by staff of the Joint Committee on Education to consider the first of five drafts of Chapter 766.[18] This group included many of those who had been involved with the Task Force for Children Out of School and with the Massachusetts Advisory Council on Education, who remained well-informed advocates for change after publication of their reports. It also included representatives of some parent groups whose initial distrust of any effort to back away from a strictly categorical approach had to be overcome. In response to these concerns, reform advocates argued that under the proposed legislation *all* groups would stand to benefit and none would have to sacrifice any presumed advantage. Legislative staff were firmly committed to a process of drafting the bill that assured that all interests would be heard and, as far as possible, accommodated.

This first meeting of the Coalition for Special Education marked the beginning of an intensive lobbying effort carefully orchestrated by committee staff. After the October meeting the coalition quickly took on a life of its own. It included among its membership representatives of thirty-three constituent organizations who, despite differences among them, shared a commitment to reform legislation.[19]

Speaker Bartley was approached to cosponsor the bill. His sponsorship was considered crucial, since the few bills he sponsored were backed heavily and with considerable success. Following a favorable recommendation by his staff Bartley agreed to cosponsor the bill, and it was filed in December 1971.[20]

Members of the coalition, backed by staff support from the Joint Committee on Education, then initiated efforts to secure the support of other legislators. These efforts included letter writing, telephone campaigns, and personal visits. While the evidence is not altogether clear on this point, some observers suggested that initial cost estimates of the Department of Education and Joint Committee on Education—$10 million per year—were intentionally conservative to avoid scaring off cost-conscious legislators.[21] In fact, Speaker Bartley himself later claimed that he was "misled on the cost."[22]

An additional factor that may have influenced the legislature to act quickly on special education reform was a class-action suit that had been filed in September 1970 and was still pending in 1972. The suit (Stewart v. Phillips) had been filed against the state departments of education and mental health and the Boston school department, challenging the misuse of IQ tests with low-income and minority children, the consequent misclassification of children in special classes for the retarded, and the denial of regular school services to children placed in such classes.[23] The example of Pennsylvania, where special education reform policies were adopted in settlement of a suit in October 1971, was well known to special education interest groups in Massachusetts.[24] The coalition made certain that legislators were aware that the same thing could happen in Massachusetts should they fail to act.

The only major source of opposition to Chapter 766 came from private school operators who feared a loss of students and revenue if the law were implemented. Their concerns led to the inclusion of a grandfather clause specifying that children already placed in private schools as of September 1974 would be permitted to remain as long as their parents so desired. In addition, a requirement was added at their insistence that a review board be appointed to examine implementing regulations for Chapter 766 before their promulgation by the Massachusetts Department of Education.[25]

The Department of Mental Health, while not opposed to the intent of the bill, favored itself over the Department of Education as the agency responsible for administering the proposed law. In April 1972 the Republican governor, Francis Sargent, submitted to the Democratic-controlled legislature his own special education bill. It differed from the Bartley-Daly version chiefly in proposing the Department of Mental Health for the primary administrative role. Sargent later withdrew the bill and supported Chapter 766.[26]

Public school administrators also supported its intent, restricting their expressed opposition in some cases to statements that the law was unnecessary since they were already doing what the law would require in their current special education programs.[27] The Massachusetts Teachers Association took a guarded stance, coming out neither strongly for nor against.[28] The state's leading newspaper, the *Boston Globe*, supported the bill editorially and provided extensive coverage of events leading to its introduction and ultimate passage. It was passed in July 1972 by unanimous voice vote of both chambers of the legislature. The governor quickly signed it into law.

The Implementation Context

The response of local school systems was conditioned in large measure by what transpired at the state level following passage of Chapter 766. Several conditions favored successful implementation. The process of generating support for its passage led to the formation of an organization, the Coalition for Special Education, that remained committed to the full and early implementation of the bill after it was passed.[29]

The careful research by committee staff and the drafting and redrafting of the bill with involvement of all interested sectors yielded a clear and concise piece of legislation—a strong law that spelled out what was to be done, when, how, and by whom. It also provided two years of lead time for planning and preparation before the schools had to put the law into effect, additional resources to restructure the state education agency to assume a more active leadership role in implementation, clear and detailed regulations, and plans for both constituent monitoring and state oversight of local effort.[30]

Clear and Detailed Regulations

In December 1972 the Division of Special Education convened ten task forces, consisting of 252 persons representing parent and professional groups and others interested in the law, and charged each task force with drafting a section of the regulations. The regulations went through three full drafts and were the subject of public hearings held throughout the state. The result was a 107-page single-spaced set of regulations that has been described as "among the most specific and stringent ever adopted for any public education program, state or federal."[31]

Lead Time for Planning and Preparation

There was an overriding concern for rapid implementation from parent and advocacy groups matched by an equally strong conservatism among state and local school officials who favored postponing implementation even beyond the two-year planning period. Yet the fact remains that the law provided a full two-year period to plan and prepare for the program's implementation. While this time might have been used to better advantage, much was accomplished during this period. The regulations were developed with an unprecedented degree of input from virtually all interested parties. The Department of Education had an opportunity to begin planning and reorganizing to assume a changed role. Local school systems had two years in which to contemplate the local implications of the legislation and to develop their plans for its implementation. And consumer groups and the education department undertook a major campaign to inform parents and teachers of the provisions of Chapter 766.[32]

Resources for Building Organizational Capacity

A key element in undertaking complex and innovative special education reform is the capacity of the state education bureaucracy to plan, coordinate, mobilize support for, direct, monitor, and assess its implementation. When the Massachusetts Special Education Law was passed in July 1972, the Department of Education was ill-suited to the active leadership required. The school governance system in Massachusetts is among the most decentralized in the nation, reflecting a strong tradition of localism and a revenue-raising system heavily dependent on the local property tax. In FY1975, 70 percent of school revenues were raised locally.[33] In 1972 there were few slack resources that could be mobilized, and the incumbent staff of the Division of Special Education was small and imbued with a reactive style toward local education authorities, as was typical of many state departments of education. In addition, the Division of Special Education enjoyed the low status until recently associated with special education efforts.[34]

However, these deficits were recognized, and the opportunity was provided to transform the division into the active agency necessary to give leadership in implementing the new law. There was slightly more than two years' lead time during which the division could ready itself for the added responsibilities. The budget of the division was more than doubled, from $350,000 for 1973 to $800,000 for 1974, making available twenty-nine new staff positions.[35] These resources offered the potential for the critical mass necessary for a rapid transformation of the division to an active leadership role. The status of the division was upgraded by elevating its head from assistant to associate commissioner in December 1972. The potential for a reorientation of the division was further increased through the fortuitous resignation of the associate commissioner, Joseph Rice, and his replacement in August 1974 by Robert Audette. Low salary scales and cumbersome procedures for getting specific positions approved and individuals hired in the state system continued to constitute a serious obstacle to rapid transformation of the division. However, the use of federal grants for contract services provided a means amply used by the division to recruit assistance for short-term tasks on short notice.

Oversight and Monitoring of Performance

The division had made it known that it intended to give priority to monitoring and evaluating local compliance with the law. Local education authorities were required to submit plans for division approval, showing how they intended to carry out the law. A new state agency, the Office for Children, was established to coordinate, monitor, and assess services for children. The agency was to serve as an advocate for children's interests and was assigned oversight responsibility for Chapter 766.[36] Within the division a new unit, the Bureau of Child Advocacy, was established to process appeals brought by parents challenging school actions under Chapter 766. The Massachusetts Advocacy Center, the successor organization to the Task Force for Children Out of School, and the Coalition for Special Education jointly announced plans for monitoring Chapter 766 compliance in each locality throughout the state. This monitoring effort, while flawed by the reporting of some inaccurate data, served as a prior restraint for local special education administrators, who in general reacted with almost paranoid horror at the thought of having an outside group of noneducators examine their performance.[37]

The meetings of the special education directors' group, the Association of Administrators for Special Education, invariably included one or more disdainful references to advocacy groups, which usually meant the Massachusetts Advocacy Center and the Coalition for Special Education. A cartoon circulated at one meeting showed a Frankenstein monster, labeled "Massachusetts Ch. 766 Regs." coming to life while two "mad" scientists labeled "Advocacy Groups" and "Boston Bureaucrats" congratulated each other. The caption read, "Damned if we won't win the 'Innovation of the Decade' award."

Implementation Constraints

While auspicious implementation conditions existed, three problems contributed to local implementation difficulties: poor planning and management on the part of the Division of Special Education; continued uncertainty throughout the two-year planning period about what would be required of local schools, and when;

and perhaps most serious of all, failure of the legislature to guarantee adequate funding. These conditions exacerbated work load pressures within the schools and at the same time amplified discretion at the local level, thereby contributing to unintended distortions in carrying out the law.

Much of the chaos observed during the first year's operation is attributable to poor planning and management on the part of the state Department of Education. The development of the regulations illustrate the confusion that characterized Division of Special Education planning. The staffing and coordination lacked direction. There were no guidelines from the division, and (according to one task force chairperson) the ten citizen task forces charged with drafting the regulations wasted considerable time developing overlapping and conflicting content. Robert Audette, the newly appointed associate commissioner of the division, complained of the process under his predecessor, "By October 1973 they were so far behind it was pathetic."[38] The regulations went through three complete revisions and were not issued until March 1974, three months *after* the time when school committees across the state were preparing budgets for the spring town meetings.[39]

The regulations set forth in detail what the schools were required to do; they did not say, however, how the schools were to carry out these requirements. Such specification of the activities to be undertaken by school systems is ordinarily prescribed in administrative guidelines. The division in fact allocated considerable time, effort, and expense ($146,000) to the development by an outside consultant of an operations manual for the individualized education program procedures called core evaluations.[40] The product, unveiled to harried local special education administrators some ten weeks *after* the beginning of the 1974–75 school year, proved so complex and unwieldy that its use was made optional in response to vociferous protest. The development of the statewide Association of Administrators for Special Education was in direct response to the requirement that the Core Evaluation Manual and its twenty-six new forms be used in the assessment process. At the first meeting of this new organization, angry administrators actually considered a mass manual-burning on the State House steps.[41]

Another contract for the development of a manual for administrators was not executed until June 1974, for delivery by December 31, again some three and a half months after the Chapter 766 implementation date.[42] When it was completed, the division found it necessary to set up a committee of special education administrators to revise the manual and bring it into line with the realities of local program administration.

While the availability of federal funds permitted contracting with individuals and consulting firms for short-term planning activities, the success of such efforts was largely contingent on the quality of oversight from the division. As the experience with the core evaluation manual illustrates, the coordination and oversight of consultant activities left much to be desired. There were frequent misunderstandings about how projects were to be financed. A public relations project using several consulting firms to sensitize the state to the implications of Chapter 766 was submitted by one unit of the division for final contract approval; it was then learned that funds for the same activity had already been allocated to the Office for Children. Considerable staff work went into arranging agreements with organizations across the state to provide in-service training for teachers. This program, too, had to be abandoned when it was learned that the money earmarked for this purpose had been allocated to another organization. Even within the division, something as trivial as the content of a transparency to be used in a workshop sometimes took months to be approved.[43]

Attempts by school administrators and even regional staff of the division to secure policy clarifications were usually frustrated. By June 1974 the division was flooded with questions about Chapter 766. The regional offices were unable to provide answers because of protracted delay in making policy decisions at the division, and calls to the division were frequently "lost" because the secretarial staff did not know to whom they should be referred. Policy decisions that were made were resolved on an ad hoc basis by the associate commissioner with advice of counsel and were not always communicated to the bureau directors. The situation was not addressed until January 1975 when an eighteen-member policy group was appointed.[44]

It is ironic that poor management could be attributed to the nation's first state department of education. Yet the Massachusetts department, not unlike most other state departments of education, had long maintained a more or less passive stance on local systems.[45] This stance had changed but slightly with the increase of federal funds for education in the 1960s. The state education department had a reputation among local administrators as inefficient, dominated by Boston interests, and having, until the advent of Chapter 766, let the local systems "work things out for themselves."[46]

The state commissioner for education and legislative leaders recognized the need for change. The legislature provided for an upgrading of the assistant commissioner for special education position to that of associate commissioner, more than doubled the division's budget, and provided for its decentralization into six regional offices.[47] Yet even the energetic young associate commissioner, Robert Audette, who was promoted to that post from director of program development in August 1974, was limited by his own and the division's lack of managerial expertise, his firm commitment to a regulatory rather than technical assistance role for the division, and the necessity to rely on incumbent staff socialized to the old laissez-faire style. He was further hampered by a long cumbersome process for bringing in new staff and a low salary scale. These factors contributed to his recruitment of an enthusiastic but inexperienced staff seen by local school officials as "antischool" (many were recruited from the staff of Fernald, a state institution) and the reliance on outside consulting firms such as that responsible for the Core Evaluation Manual fiasco.[48]

Several of the problems within the Department of Education and Division of Special Education may be directly attributed to the inevitable disorder in launching a major new program. Yet five years later a special task force reported to the Massachusetts House Ways and Means Committee as follows:

There is a flurry of activity throughout the Department, but there are questionable gains. . . . There is a high level of staff turnover and staff turnaround in the Division of Special Education. In the past two years, most of the various bureaus have had several directors. Many of the key staff people at the central office are not even state employees at all. They are paid out of federal grants housed in private agencies or educational collaboratives, even though at times they supervise other state employees. Under such circumstances, uniform policy becomes not only difficult but improbable.[49]

Of the regional decentralization of the Department of Education, the report notes that they "have most of the responsibility but very little of the authority. They are often bypassed and often cannot provide school systems with consistent answers to their questions."[50]

Planning for Implementation

The two-year delay in implementation—the bill was signed into law in July 1972, to take effect September 1974—intended by the legislature for planning and preparation was not used to full advantage. This failure was due not only to ineffective management practices but also to uncertainty about whether full implementation would in fact be required in September 1974. A postponement until September 1975 or a gradual or phased implementation was advocated at times during the planning period by the governor, the commissioner for education, the Association of School Superintendents, and even House Speaker David Bartley and Representative Michael Daly, the prime sponsors of the bill. Parent and advocacy groups strongly opposed phasing or postponement and threatened to file suit if anything less than full implementation were approved.[51]

The debate over phasing continued until May 1974 when Speaker Bartley, faced with the certainty of a suit, withdrew his amendment permitting a gradual implementation over a three-year period. The possibility of delayed implementation undoubtedly caused many school officials to postpone gearing up for Chapter 766 pending a resolution of this crucial issue. As late as three months before the required implementation and one month before the schools closed for summer vacation, with many of those responsible for implementation due to go on summer leave, there was still much uncertainty about what the schools would be required to do, and when.[52]

Fiscal Constraints

School officials also faced uncertainty about the funding of Chapter 766. The law provides state support for local special education costs that exceed a school system's average per-pupil costs (subject to a maximum of 110 percent of the statewide average for similar special education programs). No system may receive less from the state than under the previous formulas which provided reimbursement of a flat 50 percent for most categories of children in special education programs. What seemed to be an adequate assumption by the state of new local special education costs was in fact not so generous.[53]

State reimbursement is normally distributed in November following the school year in which the funds have been expended. This means that the school system first has to raise and expend the funds and then wait for state reimbursement. In the case of Chapter 766, which was likely to increase costs considerably, this procedure would mean a substantial increase in local property taxes to pay for the new and expanded services. (Under Massachusetts law the school committees are autonomous; once they set the school budget, the town is obliged to raise the necessary revenues.)

To complicate matters further, statewide estimates of the projected first-year costs varied from the Department of Education's $40 million to the local town and school officials' $100 million.[54] In fact, no one could predict the costs with certainty since schools could not know how many children would be referred and evaluated or what specific services they would require. Furthermore, they did not know which specific special education costs would be reimbursed under Chapter 766. The necessary fiscal guidelines were not issued by the department until May 18, 1977.[55]

In April 1974 the legislature finally responded to pressure from the towns by allocating $26 million in advance funding to help the school systems finance the initial year of Chapter 766.[56] This money was not "new"; it was an advance against the reimbursement the systems would normally receive in November 1975. This up-front money, as it was called, only postponed the funding problem. The real catch was that the legislature had never fully funded the regular state aid to education program. In the previous year, for example, localities received only 81.2 percent of what they were entitled to under the law. The implications were that schools could expect to receive full state special education reimbursements; however, in the absence of greatly increased allocations by the legislature, which was unlikely, these funds would be deducted from or "taken off the top" of the regular education reimbursements. In other words, local school officials feared that while expenditures for mandated special education services would escalate, the total state education reimbursements were likely to remain at about the same level and would simply be divided differently, with more going to special education and less to regular education programs. The towns would still have to raise property taxes to cover the increased costs—an unhappy prospect in a state that was already financing 75 percent of its education costs through property taxes, a proportion exceeded by only two other states.[57] As the state secretary of administration and finance characterized the situation, "Coming up with this kind of program without financial backing is a fraud."[58]

Local school officials then faced two kinds of uncertainty; they could not know exactly how much Chapter 766 would cost, and they could not reliably predict how much or which of these costs would be reimbursed.

As subsequent events demonstrated, this uncertainty over fiscal arrangements proved beneficial to the wealthier districts. One observer working at that time in the Division of Special Education characterized the Chapter 766 funding formula as "obscure and uninterpreted" in its failure to define reimbursable costs. The Division of Special Education had nothing to do with the local school financial reporting formats. These formats were the responsibility of another Department of Education section whose staff was unfamiliar with the 766 regulations. However, the local directors of special education in the more sophisticated communities were quite familiar with the regulations, funding formula, and reporting formats, and they used this knowledge to their advantage.[59]

Discussion

Passage of the Massachusetts Comprehensive Special Education Act was made possible through a combination of circumstances that included a solid background of research documenting special education abuses and outlining reform options; a nucleus of active, informed reform advocates; influential legislative sponsors; and legislative staff who played an important role in overcoming the initial concerns of some parent groups and who helped launch the Coalition for Special Education.

The possibility of court-imposed reform contributed to the passage of the law and most certainly was a factor in heading off attempts to delay its implementation. The underestimation of its cost, possibly deliberate, expedited its passage but permitted the legislature to sidestep the issue of adequate funding of its implementation.

Chapter 766 was a consumer's law. Impetus for its passage came from outside the state education bureaucracy, and the law and regulations were written in a way that suggested anticipation of noncompliance by the schools. As one individual closely involved in the drafting of the legislation put it, "It is not a law written for administrators. . . . It reflects an underlying mistrust [of them]."[60]

Consumer interests represented through the Coalition for Special Education were sufficiently strong and united to prevent any weakening of the reform effort throughout the long bargaining process that accompanied the drafting of the legislation and writing of the regulations. They also played a role in selecting Robert Audette as associate commissioner of the division. His experience was institutional rather than public school, and his approach was to emphasize regulation of local compliance rather than technical assistance. In a departure from the laissez-faire stance of the past, the division now stressed in its communications with school officials its intention to strictly monitor local compliance. This intention was reflected in requirements for prior approval for a variety of local school actions. However, the division lacked the capacity to enforce its requirements, and it subsequently relaxed them as regional offices became buried in forms which they lacked the staff resources to process. When program audits finally got under way in late 1976, they focused primarily on compliance with procedures and gave little attention to the quality of service provided by local education agencies. A legislative committee report noted that a local education agency could expect to be audited once in five years.[61]

The new regulatory approach, less than effective in improving local school performance, contributed to the belief frequently expressed by local school administrators that the division had taken an adversarial stance toward the schools. In response to requests from special education administrators that they be consulted in policy matters, Audette was quoted by an associate as saying he refused to be pressured by any group.

The two-year planning period provided by the legislature had not been fully utilized because of turnover of leadership within the division (Audette was the third head within two years), poor management, and continued uncertainty about the implementation date and about reimbursement for local effort. As of September 1974 local school officials faced the prospect of having to implement a law written with an expectation of their noncompliance, administered by a state bureaucracy they regarded as antischool, with their performance to be watched by advocacy groups whom they considered unfriendly. They were being forced to relinquish a measure of autonomy and become more accountable for their policies and actions. They were required to carry out radically different practices, many of which they considered unnecessary. Implementing guidelines were not yet ready, so they were forced to develop their own plans in the hope that they would conform to whatever requirements might subsequently be issued. These efforts would cost considerably more than current special education programs, but they could not know how much more. Reimbursement for these costs was uncertain.

The events leading to the passage of Chapter 766 in Massachusetts and subsequently to PL 94–142 at the federal level seemed to support the pluralist view of the openness of the political system to progressive social change. The widespread denial of free appropriate public education to handicapped children had gained recognition through the actions of parent groups seeking change through the courts, state legislatures, and finally Congress. Parent and advocacy groups had been aided in these efforts by sympathetic legislators and by a growing body of research supporting the need for reform of special education practices. Yet the passage of a law marks a beginning, not the end, of efforts to achieve reform objectives. What happens after the law is passed is crucial.

II
STREET-LEVEL RESPONSE

3
Translating Law into Action:
The Schools Prepare to Respond

A number of factors could be expected to affect implementation of special education reform: the law itself and the implementing regulations, the funding arrangements, external support groups, provisions for monitoring compliance, and the capacity of the state education agency to oversee the execution of the law. What actually happened at the local level as schools responded to the provisions of Chapter 766 can be seen from an examination of the performance against the requirements and intent of the law and regulations. While poor planning and underfunding contributed to implementation problems, the impact of the law on the work situations of teachers and specialists at the local level accounts to a considerable degree for the quality of school response.

The major thrust of the law, and that which makes it truly innovative, is the requirement that children with special needs receive individualized assessment and treatment. This thrust is reflected in provisions requiring that children be assessed by an interdisciplinary team with parental involvement, that a specific education program be tailored to the needs of each child, that generic descriptive labels be replaced by behaviorally specific inventories, and that children with special needs be accommodated whenever possible in regular education settings. At the same time certain provisions of the law are directed toward achieving uniform and nondiscriminatory treatment and comprehensive coverage of all children with special needs. As this discussion of local implementation will show, these two aims, individualization and comprehensiveness, are not compatible.

The Local Implementation Context

Chapter 766 assigned to local education authorities responsibility for educating all children between three and twenty-one within their geographical jurisdiction. All children with special needs were to be evaluated, have individualized education programs developed, and special services begun for them in the first year. Special outreach efforts to identify children with special needs were required. Assessment was to be accomplished within three months from referral to completion of the education program and approval of it by the parent. All these provisions were to be accomplished within a framework of procedural safeguards for due process and equitable treatment.

Such requirements were well beyond the normal capacity of most Massachusetts school systems, even under the best of circumstances. Moreover special education administrators began the 1974–75 school year without specific guidelines for constituting assessment teams, evaluating children, and writing education programs. The regulations stipulated what needed to be done but provided no blueprint for administering the process. The Division of Special Education and organized parent groups had taken an adversarial stance toward local schools; as a result, administrators feared numerous court suits and appeals by parents which they believed they would lose. Parents were for the first time to be directly involved in educational planning for their own children, thereby challenging the autonomy of education professionals. Schools were being required to provide social, psychological, and medical services that many educators believed to be well beyond the legitimate purview of educational institutions. There was doubt that full state reimbursement would in fact be available to pay for such services, and the anticipated competition for resources within school systems threatened to exacerbate underlying tensions between regular and special education personnel. Furthermore, for each step taken in implementing the law numerous forms had to be completed, creating an enormous paperwork burden.

The Core Evaluation Process

The drastic impact of the law on local systems is illustrated by procedures for evaluating and arranging services for children. Before Chapter 766 a specialist simply started working with a child after consulting informally with the teacher and parent and perhaps administering some diagnostic tests. The principal, other specialists, and the appropriate supervisor might or might not also be consulted, depending on the nature of the problem and the custom of that school system and school. Even the assignment of a child to a special class was often handled with similar informality. Under Chapter 766 what had been a simple procedure became a major team undertaking, with elaborate requirements governing each step along the way.

The process in Massachusetts officially begins with the completion of a referral form. (Referrals may be initiated by a parent, teacher or other school official, court or social agency.) Before that, however, "all efforts shall be made to meet such children's needs within the context of the services which are part of the regular education program,"[1] and the referral must document the efforts that have been tried. Within five days after the referral is initiated, a written notice is sent to the parents informing them of the types of assessment to be conducted, when the evaluation will begin, and their right to participate in all meetings in which the education plan is being developed.[2] In addition to the written notice, parents have the right to meet with the chairperson of the evaluation team to receive an explanation of the reason for the evaluation and the way the process will be carried out. The parent must give written consent to the evaluation and its individual components before the assessment can be initiated.

A full core evaluation is required when the child is expected to be placed outside the regular class more than 25 percent of the time. For a full core evaluation all the following assessments must be completed:

1. "An assessment of the child's educational status by an administrative representative of the school department."
2. An assessment by a recent or current teacher of "the child's specific behavioral abilities along a developmental continuum, . . . school readiness, functioning, or achievement, . . . behavioral adjustment, attentional capacity, motor coordination, activity level and patterns, communication skills, memory, and social relations with groups, peers and adults."
3. "A comprehensive health assessment, by a physician."
4. "An assessment by a psychologist, including an individually appropriate psychological examination, . . . a developmental and social history, observation of the child in familiar surroundings (such as a classroom), sensory, motor, language, perceptual, attentional, cognitive, affective, attitudinal, self-image, interpersonal, behavioral, interest, and vocational factors."

5. "An assessment by a nurse, social worker, or guidance or adjustment counselor of pertinent family history and home situation factors including . . . a home visit."
6. Additional assessments by psychiatric, neurological, learning disability, speech, hearing, vision, motor, or any other specialists, as
required.[3]

For each assessment, a detailed, written report of the findings
must be forwarded to the team chairperson and frequently to the
specialist's supervisor as well. After the individual assessments are
completed, team members may choose to come together in a
"precore" meeting to discuss their findings. Finally, there is another
team meeting, with parents, in which the education plan is developed. The education plan is to include a specific statement of what
the child can and cannot do, the child's learning style, and educational goals and plans for meeting them for the following three, six,
and nine months.[4] This entire process, starting from the day the
notification letter is mailed to the parents and ending with the
completion of the educational plan, is to take no more than thirty
days.

Community and School System Characteristics

Since I wished to compare the response of several school systems to
the requirements of the new law, I selected systems for study that
shared some common characteristics. My intention was not to carry
out a systematic comparison of school systems but to study a range
of examples. I hypothesized that even similar school systems would
differ in their administrative response but that common coping
patterns would be observed at the street level.

There is a wide disparity among Massachusetts towns in relative
wealth and in expenditures for education. The mean community
wealth per child in 1974 for communities in the highest quintile was
$150,055; the mean for the lowest quintile was $26,957.[5] The average
per-pupil expenditure in 1975 was $1335, but the range was from less
than $700 to more than $2500.[6]

I deliberately chose to study school systems that ranked among
the highest in community wealth, because I wished to avoid biasing

the study by examining school systems whose poverty of resources would expose them to the most severe implementation problems. The three systems are among the largest in the state; each serves an urban community of over 50,000 population. None of these communities has a nonwhite population greater than 10 percent. Two of the systems also ranked among the highest in the state in per-pupil expenditures. The three are all located in the greater Boston metropolitan area, belong to the same educational planning collaborative, and are served by the same regional office of the Division of Special Education. A comparison of community and school system characteristics is shown in table 1.

Table 1
Community and School Characteristics

	System A	System B	System C
Approximate Enrollment*	6,000	10,000	11,000
Per-Pupil Expenditures	$2,200	$1,850	$1,218
Pupil-Teacher Ratio (Elementary)	16	15	20
Median Family Income	$14,000	$10,000	$11,000
Percentage of Professional, Technical, Managerial Workers in Community	45%	39%	22%
Approximate Wealth per School-Age Child	$101,000	$75,000	$59,000
Quintile Rank in State, Wealth per Child	I	I	II
Reimbursements for Special Education Divided by Total Enrollment	$69	$137	$112
Quintile Rank in State, Special Education Reimbursements per Child Enrolled	I	I	I

Sources: Family income and employment status figures are based on 1970 census data; and enrollment and pupil-teacher ratios are based on 1972 school reports, as listed in the "City and Town Monograph" series, Massachusetts Department of Commerce and Development, July 1973. Per-pupil expenditures, wealth per child, and special education reimbursements are from David M. Sheehan, "The Children's Puzzle," Boston, Mass.: Institute for Governmental Research, University of Massachusetts, 1977, appendix B.
*The statistics have been stated as approximations to discourage identification of the school systems.

While similar in some respects, the three school systems differed significantly in terms of the communities served, the expenditures for education, and their administrative styles. System A serves a more highly professional and affluent community and spends more on education than the other two. It also enjoys a reputation as a highly professionalized system not shared by the others to the same degree, although all three systems are highly regarded by professional educators throughout the state. While hard data on the relative professionalization of the three systems are difficult to develop, this characterization of system A can be supported in several ways. In systems B and C, one's place of origin and current residence was a factor weighed in personnel recruitment and selection, particularly for administrative posts; preference, unofficially at least, was given to candidates who could demonstrate some attachment to the town. In system B, according to several informants, certain positions were informally allocated to those of Irish background. Such a parochial outlook was not evident in system A. By contrast, personnel in system A spoke with considerable pride of the quality of staff, including many with Ph.D.'s, recruited nationally. Several administrators in system A held positions of leadership in their respective national professional organizations. The system has been among the first in the country to establish a number of new programs and facilities, and several of its special programs have been the subject of laudatory articles in national publications.

The three systems also approached the September 1974 starting date with greatly differing staff resources and contrasting prior experiences in special education programming. All three systems reported increased special education expenditures in the year prior to implementation of Chapter 766. Systems A and C reported spending about 25 percent more for special education programs in the 1973–74 school year than in the previous year. System B increased its special education spending by nearly 60 percent.[7]

While there is no direct evidence on this, the increases in special education expenditures in the 1973–74 school year (prior to the required implementation for Chapter 766) may have been made in response to a provision of the law's funding formula. Beginning with the 1974–75 school year, the state reimbursed all special education costs, over and above regular education costs, to a maximum of 110 percent of the state average per-pupil expenditure for special education. This feature of the so-called equalizing formula imposed a ceiling on reimbursements to high-spending districts. However, special education reimbursements until 1979 could not be less than those for 1972 and 1973 under a "hold-harmless" provision of the law. This provided a powerful incentive for the wealthier districts to increase their special education spending during these two years so that they would not be subject to the 110 percent ceiling. Wilken and Porter found that "many districts did increase their expenditure very dramatically during [1972-74] in part with the intention of building a base for the next 5 years."[8] Systems A and B were in the highest quintile in special education expenditures and would clearly have benefited from building a higher spending base.

Table 2 shows how the systems compared at the end of the 1973-74 school year with respect to staff and expenditures for special education and the numbers of pupils then receiving special education services.

The variation between systems was substantial. System C, the

Table 2
Special Education Staff, Expenditures, and Enrollment (1973-74)

	System A	System B	System C
Staff	23	257	76
Expenditures	$402,815	$2,386,107	$911,329
Pupils Served	257	1,590	1,247
Percentage of Total Enrollment Served	4.2	16.1	10.7
Expenditures per Pupil Served*	$1,567	$1,501	$731
Number of Pupils per Staff Member	11.2	6.2	16.4
Percentage of Pupils Fully Integrated**	58.0	88.7	82.3

Source: Department of Education, Division of Special Education, "Claim for State Aid to Special Education Programs, Chapters 69 and 71, Amended," form SPED 5, for the years ending June 30, 1973, and June 30, 1974. These reports served as the basis for state reimbursement for special education expenditures.
*The total special education expenditures reported divided by the number of pupils served.
**These are pupils in a regular class program at least 75 percent of the time.

least affluent, was reaching a percentage of its enrollment 2.5 times that of system A, the richest of the three. The percentage served by system B was nearly four times as great as system A. However, these data say nothing of the appropriateness or quality of services for children with special needs.

Both systems A and B reported spending double that of system C. While systems A and B were spending at a comparable rate, system B reported a much richer staff-pupil ratio. Nearly 90 percent of those served in system B were in fully integrated programs, but only 58 percent of those in system A were. These data suggest that system A tended to concentrate its special education resources on a lesser number of children with more intensive services, whereas both systems B and C spread their resources over a much larger proportion of the student body.

Again these differences may reflect different strategies in response to the Chapter 766 reimbursement formula. Special education (Chapter 766) and regular education (Chapter 70) reimbursements are funded from the same appropriation and constitute a fixed amount. However, Chapter 70 has never been fully funded by the state. Since Chapter 766 is prior-funded, meaning that the state must pay all special education claims before paying regular education claims, an increase in Chapter 766 reimbursements means a decrease in Chapter 70 aid. Chapter 70 has an equalizing formula that provides substantially less to rich districts than to poor ones.

Hence, to the extent that rich districts can shift pupils from regular class programs to special class programs, they can receive increasing amounts of state aid, and the more this shifting occurs, the greater the draw against Chapter 70 funds to be distributed for basic equalization purposes, and the smaller the supply of basic equalization becomes, the more it works to the detriment of poor communities.[9]

A task force reporting to the Massachusetts House Ways and Means Committee put it this way:

It is no secret in the Commonwealth that wealthier communities increase their state aid by shifting expenditures to the more lucrative Chapter 766 formula for reimbursement. . . . The wide disparity between wealthy and poor communities has not been closed by the "equalizing" formula of Chapter 70; in fact, the formula is de-equalizing and the reimbursement formula for Chapter 766 further compounds the problem.[10]

It became quite clear during my field study in the 1974–75 school year that system B was pursuing a strategy to maximize the number of children in special education programs, but why they were doing so was not then clear. On the other hand, system A sought to keep the number of children in special education to a minimum, and I can only surmise that their fiscal officer failed to appreciate the subtleties of the reimbursement formula.[11]

Organizing the Core Evaluation Teams

Given the differences among local school systems, the absence of specific guidance from the Division of Special Education, and a strong New England tradition of localism which inhibited a sharing of their plans, one would expect local responses to the law to differ.[12] This was indeed the case, as is exemplified by differing approaches to the core evaluation (individualized education plan) process. Any number of models of core evaluation team would have been consistent with the regulations. These are approaches taken by the three systems.

System A
System A, with the smallest enrollment, designated a psychologist, social worker, and learning disabilities specialist already on staff as the primary core evaluation team (CET). Several additional part-time specialists were hired to supplement this team, and existing school-based specialists and teachers were brought in as needed to participate in the evaluations. This school system has a strong tradition of principal and school autonomy and professionalism. Although the primary team did conduct most of the evaluations in the central·district headquarters offices, many evaluations were done in the schools, sometimes without participation of any of the primary team members, resulting in a two-tier system of assessment. One can argue that the ownership of the assessment process by local school-based personnel may engender a greater commitment to the outcome, but in this instance it appeared that decisions to follow or ignore the requirements of the law were frequently made at the individual school level without consultation from the central staff.

The team and administrators adopted a largely reactive and defensive stance toward the evaluation process. Their records were maintained haphazardly, and in contrast to systems B and C there was little organized follow-up to assure completion of referrals. Lost records were a frequent concern. Except for referrals generated through prekindergarten and kindergarten screening and the generally routine pro forma evaluation of children already in special classes, the team simply processed referrals coming to them. That is, in contrast to systems B and C, there was minimal organized effort to generate referrals from teachers and principals; in fact, some principals were advised by administrators to cut back on referrals in order to conserve funds. This informal policy resulted in a relatively high proportion of outside referrals; about half the evaluations completed during the year resulted from parent or agency referrals. (The comparable figure for both systems B and C was about 15 percent.) The reactive posture was rationalized by personnel at all levels with the argument that most children with special needs were already being served and that the quality of services was superior to that found in most other school systems.

System B
System B had hired an outside business consultant to design a system for central oversight of the work flow. New forms and written procedures were developed for personnel involved at each step of the referral and evaluation process. Central files made it possible to determine which forms were outstanding for any particular child, and follow-up procedures were instituted to assure completion of the education plan process. On the whole, the record keeping was excellent.

Assessment and education plans were forwarded to administrative supervisors to provide central control over their quality. An aggressive case-finding effort was undertaken through screening and orientation of teachers and principals. School psychologists were designated as chairpersons of the core evaluation teams, with responsibility for several schools each. Their numbers were doubled to accommodate this added work load. (They still retained responsibility for testing children.) The balance of the team consisted of other school-based specialists. Administrators rarely attended assessment meetings.

An administrator stated that extreme care had been taken to follow the letter of the law, since a vociferous minority of parents would be likely to grasp any error and make an issue of it with the school committee (school board). The school committee was highly politicized, and even the most routine matters became the subject of heated and rancorous debate. This system tended to be dominated by a concern for completing the forms properly and speedily, with the result that assessment meetings were conducted hastily and with a minimum of genuine deliberation.

System C

In system C, the largest of the three but with the smallest per-pupil expenditures, the personal involvement in most of the evaluations of the special education administrator or one of the program directors assured a high degree of quality control. They viewed their participation as a means to train school-based staff through their example and interactions in the meetings. The evaluations were regarded as belonging to the schools, and the core evaluation teams were chaired by a much more varied array of personnel than in the other systems.

The administrators prided themselves on having direct acquaintance with most of the cases referred for evaluation—no small task, considering that 330 were completed during the year. This personal approach was symbolized by a roster of names and dates of children referred, indicating the stage of each evaluation, on the blackboard in the administrator's office (probably in violation of confidentiality provisions of the law). The record-keeping system was developed by the administrator and her secretarial staff and, while lacking the sophistication of system B's, was adequate.

The relatively new superintendent and his assistant had been trying to imbue staff at all levels with a philosophy emphasizing individualization of instruction and the creation of an environment conducive to learning. They supported Chapter 766 as furthering these goals. The assistant superintendent held biweekly meetings with special education administrative and supervisory staff and generally supported their efforts to improve and increase special education services. He did not hesitate to ask the school committee for increased funds for such purposes although frequently at a lesser level than special education staff requested. These requests reflected his sense of what the school committee would accept. For example, during most of the first year, the full-time staff was increased by only one psychologist, and the limited number of psychologists available for testing created a severe bottleneck in the processing of referrals.

Whereas in systems A and B the education plans were developed by staff in precore evaluation meetings usually held without the parents' presence, system C held far fewer of these precore meetings. The regulations state that parents "have the right to be present at and participate in *all* meetings of the CET where the educational plan is being developed and written."[13] The usual practice in system C was to hold just one meeting with parents in attendance, with the outcome still problematic. As a result, these meetings tended to be characterized by a great deal of give-and-take, a high level of parent involvement, and genuine group problem solving. Their deliberations were longer, with more people involved, and they conducted a much higher percentage of full core, as contrasted with intermediate, evaluations.

The requirements of Chapter 766 presented school personnel with an enormous increase in their work load in several ways. There were suddenly many more children to be evaluated. For each evaluation many more individuals had to be involved, and each assessment and education program had to be written in much greater detail, completed faster, and circulated to a wider audience than before. Getting everyone together for a team meeting, when each team member had a unique work schedule and many additional responsibilities, became a major task in itself. Someone, usually the chairperson, had to make provision for a meeting room, frequently a corner of the library or an anteroom in the often-crowded schools. Arrangements had to be made to have parents and team members come; substitutes had to be scheduled so that classroom teachers could attend. An evaluation of a child that might previously have taken two or three people a few hours to complete now took as much as ten to twenty hours for the chairperson and two to six hours for each of the other team members. Time previously spent working with children was now allocated to paperwork and meetings.

Their individual approaches differed, yet all three systems shared requirements for radically altered evaluation practices, an overwhelming increase in work load, and concerns about monitoring of their activities by the Division of Special Education, advocacy groups, and individual parents distrustful of their willingness and capability to comply. How they carried out the evaluations under these circumstances is the subject of the next chapter.

4
Parent Participation and School Authority:
Who Shall Speak for the Children?

Chapter 766 and PL 94–142 both call for an individualized approach to educating children. However, the work situations of educators and the requirement for comprehensiveness create strong pressures for mass processing. This tension between individualization and mass processing is not unique; it is characteristic of many street-level bureaucracies that attempt to reconcile individualized service with high demand relative to resources. Since street-level bureaucracies, particularly schools, may not officially restrict intake, other means must be found to accommodate the work load.

In the case of special education in the past, these work load pressures were at least partly responsible for many of the abuses reform legislation was intended to correct, such as arbitrary assessment, labeling and dumping troublesome youngsters into segregated special classes, excluding or denying appropriate services to children with special needs, and inappropriately institutionalizing children who could be served in their home communities. These work load pressures did not disappear with the passage of a law; on the contrary, they increased under the substantial burden of added demands.

The core evaluation process, a central component of Chapter 766, offered an opportunity to examine the impact of both increased and altered work load demands on decision making by school personnel. It also provided a setting in which to observe how specialists and administrators related to parents, teachers, and one another while deciding the fate of individual children.

Between January and June 1975, I observed forty of these assessment meetings, and the nature of parent-school interactions observed in the evaluation process is the subject of this chapter. I shall also discuss more generally how street-level bureaucrats coped with a drastically increased work load.[1]

School personnel put forth extraordinary effort to comply with the new demands. However, there was simply no way that everything required could be done with the resources available. Their behavior does not so much reflect negatively on school personnel as it demonstrates how new demands are accommodated into the work structure of people who must consistently find ways of conserving resources and asserting priorities to meet the demands of their jobs.

The Core Evaluation Process: The Ideal and the Reality

A parent, teacher or other school official, or a representative of a court or social agency who suspects that a child may need special education services may make a referral for an evaluation. Once a referral has been initiated and the parent has given permission to proceed, the school system is obliged to conduct an assessment within thirty days. The assessment, performed by an interdisciplinary team, brings together information about the home situation, class performance, intellectual functioning, emotional adjustment, and skills of the child. The use of standardized tests to determine physical, emotional, and intellectual functioning and to diagnose problems is an integral part of the procedure; so are assessments based on observation in the classroom, a home visit or interview with the parent, and a pooling of information from those who are most familiar with the child. Finally team members meet with the parents and the child (if the child is old enough) and, based on the findings, develop an education program tailored to the child's specific needs. The central concern throughout the process is the needs of the child. The team is to make its plans unconstrained by costs or even current availability of services, as it is the responsibility of the special education administrator to see that the plan is implemented even if it requires starting new programs.

This is the ideal. The observations of core evaluations demonstrated that in fact this frequently happens. Parents join with teachers and other professionals to assess the child's problem and prescribe a plan. More frequently, perhaps, the core evaluation team meeting with the parent serves as an almost ritualistic certification of the child's status—of having "special needs"—and a recitation to the parent of decisions already made by school officials.[2]

The parents are at a great disadvantage in these meetings. They are outnumbered. They enter a meeting, frequently in a strange room, where they confront a number of people, many for the first time. They are usually outsiders joining an ongoing group; the core evaluation team has generally met together as a group during previous assessments, and its members work together on a continuing basis. Parents may confront a subtle (sometimes not so subtle) implication that the child and parent are somehow at fault for creating a problem. This is particularly true when the problem is disruptive behavior or a learning difficulty whose nature is not readily apparent. Often there are status differences where a poor or working-class parent faces a group of middle-class professionals, presumed experts in their respective fields, who dress differently and speak a different language.

The Aura of Science

The use of technical jargon lends an aura of science to the proceedings while making much of the discussion unintelligible to the parent and frequently to the teacher as well. Some examples follow.[3]

A psychologist explains the test results for a seventh grader. The mother and father are present. The father is a manual laborer.

We went over prior tests. Verbal, 109, high average; new learning, a component of the social situation, scale score 17; object assembly was perfect—fast, methodical, an incredible gestalt in sight and puzzle completion. Performance was 130, the top 3 percent of the population. When you have a difference between two tests like this . . . an active, aggressive, acting-out child, math low which he refused to do, no anxiety, no tension, both are 120 which puts him in the top 5 percent of the population. . . .

Here another psychologist explains test results to a parent:

He is poor in visual-motor tasks. He has come up [improved] on sequencing object assembly completions which may reflect maturation in addition to training—that is, his visual-motor improvement.

Here is an interpretation to parents of an intelligence test presented by the guidance counselor who is chairing the evaluation meeting:

An intern tested Bill last year and while it wasn't written up, his WISC was 120; that is significantly above average.

The psychologist at this point interjects:

I would question that test. Two weeks ago I gave him a Slawson on which he got a 103 which is a solid average.

The chairman of a core evaluation team tells the parent:

Sally is not performing up to expectations. Therefore, we scheduled an intermediate core. It was really no big thing. Should I list three deficits?—Auditory attention, memory, and concentration. I have a list of things that I will do to help.

The resource room teacher reporting for the learning disabilities tutor advises the parents of the same child:

Sally performed above average in most subtests. Her deficiency is not gross. She would not be seen by the learning disabilities tutor. She simply had some trouble listening in groups.

The parent picking up on the earlier use of the term "auditory attention" then asks, "Should I have her ears checked?" The speech specialist responds, "That's not a bad idea, but we don't really think that's the problem."

There follows a long discussion between the speech specialist, resource room teacher, and classroom teacher about the mechanics of having the child's ears examined, which ends with the suggestion that the parent take the child to Massachusetts General Hospital, even though all know there is a long waiting list. Completely overlooked in this discussion is the mother's attempt to make some sense of the term auditory attention.

In another assessment meeting, a psychologist tells a working-class mother, "He does have trouble with auditory encoding." The psychologist then asks the learning disability specialist to explain tests that she had administered. The learning disability specialist continues, until finally, the mother, looking quite puzzled, asks, "What does it come from?" meaning, Why does he have this problem? The reply is, "It's a perceptual skill, and it develops faster in some areas and with some kids than with others." With that explanation they continue to another subject.

Here is a psychologist explaining the results of testing on a fifteen-year-old boy:

James has an average intellectual functioning and a pleasant personality. He is somewhat sure of himself, having good eye contact. He is a perfectionist. He has been retained a couple grades, but has excellent word skills or word encoding with a grade of 14.7. Speech was 10.2; math, 6.7; oral and silent reading, 7.5. He had trouble with the coding of the WISC and trouble with fine motor skills.

It is possible that these specialists may actually have exercised restraint in their discussions with parents. When communicating with one another, the use of jargon escalates. For example, a learn-ing disabilities tutor begins, reading from a report:

Reading 2.1 level; comprehensive language skills, good; daily per-formance, erratic. He is the type of child with learning problems; he has difficulty processing short sounds, auditory sequencing, and so forth. The visual is slightly better than the auditory channel.

A language specialist continues:

In recent testing, we found the same as Mrs. C. Difficulty with short vowels; comprehension good; cooperative in testing, but not be-forehand. Last year the WISC was given for the sake of filling state requirements for the SPED form and he said to himself aloud, "Don't be too nervous." Thus the test was not too reliable. He was very nervous. The full scale was 107+, in the average range. In information and math he got low scores; high scores in visual, 15 plus, better at names than verbal tasks.

The psychologist interjects:

I am concerned because of the difference between last year's and this year's WISC. Something happened this year. This is a thirteen point decrease in intelligence. The verbal is the same, but the sub-tests are different. The general verbal was 98 to 99. Perfect perfor-mance between 119, now down to 91. Here is the draw-a-man test. [She shows the test.] It's pretty poor, has no face or feet. There is lots of anxiety and depression that comes through in the WISC and in his conversation . . . the Bender is just a little off.

This exchange may have been perfectly intelligible to those trad-ing the various test scores; but also attending this meeting were a counselor from a youth agency who was working with the child, the classroom teacher, the school nurse, the social worker, and the principal, none of whom would necessarily have had any familiarity with these tests. To admit one's ignorance in such a meeting by asking for clarification would be difficult for professionals whose respective ranking in relation to one another was unclear.

This technical language is a shared language that school psychol-ogists, learning disabilities specialists, and others administering tests understand. The use of test scores and the abstruse manner in which they are communicated serves to assure the dominance of these specialists over others in assessment meetings.[4] Such behavior contravenes the provisions of the regulations that are intended to prevent undue reliance on tests and to insure the equal weighing of developmental and observational evidence from a variety of sources.[5] It also suggests that the participation of parents in many cases simply provides symbolic reassurance of procedural fairness without substantively affecting the outcome of the proceedings. Parents frequently do not understand what is taking place in these meetings, let alone participate as equal partners in the assessment and planning for their children.

A study of IEP meetings in Connecticut schools offers additional evidence on this point. The researchers observed and recorded actions taken at team meetings and afterwards asked participating parents what had taken place. They found that:

Parents' versions of each decision component [eligibility, place-ment, program goals, and review date] were clear and accurate no more than 50 percent of the time for any of the four components, even though the parents were present at the team meeting where these decisions were rendered. . . .

Several areas of responsibility were overlooked in communicating with parents: 1) informing parents of the decisions mandated by the PT [Planning Team]; 2) timing the notice to encourage parental participation; 3) informing parents of relevant due process safe-guards; 4) documenting crucial communications in writing. . . .

Parents were unaware of the right to introduce information at the PT and were unsure of the final recommendations. Conflicts be-tween schools and the parents . . . may have been camouflaged in the lack of clarity about the decisions that had been reached.[6]

The authors concluded:

The lack of parental understanding of the PT decisions casts serious doubts on the degree to which it can be said that parents were actively involved in decision-making.[7]

Similarly an SRI International study of 150 IEP meetings in four states, including Massachusetts, found that preplanning meetings generally occurred without parents and when parents attended they usually made little contribution.[8] Nero and Associates interviewed parents, school personnel, and advocacy group representatives in thirty-one communities in still another set of four states and found educators dubious about the value of parent participation. Parents and educators alike expressed concern about the use of technical jargon that is "noncommunicative to parents." But school person-nel believed that in some cases "the costs of notification and con-sent procedures outweighed the potential benefits of parental participation" and that "educational program development should be left to the professional educator."[9]

The exclusion of parents from participating in planning and decision making need not be an inevitable consequence of the use of shared technical language by professional and semiprofessional groups or of social class differences between parents and professionals. All street-level bureaucracies must find ways to communicate with clients; how well they do it depends on the importance of such communication for the organization. If the involvement of parents is seen simply as an additional bureaucratic hurdle, necessary only to satisfy procedural requirements, it is not likely that school personnel will take the trouble to make themselves understood to parents. However, when they want to, they can.[10]

In Massachusetts I observed some instances, although infrequent, of attempts to translate terminology into a form that could be easily understood by parents and other nonspecialists. For example, a mobility tutor in system C described in detail the tests that she had administered. Some of the tests were passed around the room while the tutor explained at length the findings in a way that was easy to follow: "Sara has difficulty in relating things to her own body. She has a lot of trouble with regard to 'what I am in space.'" The tutor then showed the Draw-a-Person test, explaining, "She has a lack of body concepts and doesn't know, for example, how big she is. Also there are no basic motor skills—that is, with regard to walking backwards, on tiptoes, and so forth. She needs instruction with gross motor skills, for example, with walking."

Such careful explanations take more time, prolong the length of the meeting, and reduce the number of evaluations that can be completed in a given period. School personnel are under severe pressure to conserve time in any way possible. One way to save time is to give only cursory explanations of test procedures and results and of education programs, trusting that parents or other school personnel will ask questions if anything is unclear.

The Advocate in the Core Evaluation Process

The Chapter 766 regulations provide that a parent "shall have the right to be accompanied and represented by a person of his/her

choice" in assessment meetings. Similarly, under PL 94–142 parents
are permitted to include in IEP meetings other individuals at their
discretion.[11] These provisions permit parents to be represented by
counsel or by advocates. The Massachusetts Coalition for Special
Education, the umbrella organization representing various special
education reform interests, initiated a project during the 1974–75
school year to recruit and train volunteers to act as child advocates
accompanying parents to meetings with school officials. However,
the use of advocates was reported to be quite limited by school
officials. For example, in only one of the forty meetings observed
was a parent accompanied by an advocate. To know about and
obtain the services of an advocate required a degree of knowledge
and sophistication many parents lacked.

A study by Alan Orenstein of two Boston-area school systems,
conducted during the 1975–76 school year, revealed starkly contrasting patterns of advocacy employed by parents in a well-to-do
suburb and in a working-class community. Parents in both school
districts described their participation in core evaluation meetings as
intimidating. However, Orenstein found:

Upper-middle-class Highview [a fictitious name] parents are better
able to cope with this situation. Many are sophisticated about the
jargon and . . . are very active in supporting one another. . . . Also,
many parents are bringing advocates with them to the core meetings . . . either nonprofessional friends and relatives, or professionals
such as social workers and therapists. One social worker has actually
set up her own business—charging parents to represent them during
the core process. Sometimes parents bring lawyers to meetings. . . .
Highview parents are also making extensive use of lay advocates
trained by the citizen groups who were instrumental in passing the
law [the Coalition for Special Education].

Bridgeport parents get much less support. The Office for Children
—a state agency—does employ professional advocates who can help
them. In Bridgeport's area, there are two such advocates for three
cities with a population of nearly 30,000 school-age children. They
. . . sit in on four or five core evaluations a month with parents. They
are beginning to train lay advocates, but have not yet developed a
system which can provide much help. Interestingly, Highview parents are not using the Office for Children advocates (they get only
one or two calls a month from Highview concerning 766), while
Bridgeport parents are making only very limited use of lay advocates
trained by predominantly upper-middle-class citizen groups. In
poorer districts, there are often no effective advocacy services
—either professional or lay.[12]

The efficacy of someone acting in an advocacy role is illustrated by the following discussion that occurred when a mother came to an evaluation meeting accompanied by a friend. Both she and the friend were of working-class background, with limited formal education.

At the conclusion of the meeting, the chairperson states, "I will read the recommendations once again and see if there are any changes." She reads from a form containing the educational plan she had written during the meeting.

Mother: As far as signing it, could I bring it in tomorrow?
Chairperson: I will ask the others to sign it and you can bring it back.
Friend: What is fine motor?

The chairperson and others explain in very specific terms with a number of examples.

Friend: How much will he lose by being out of class?

Again an explanation is offered.

Friend: Will he do as well as others?

While the friend had no formal designation as an advocate, it was clearly easier for her to ask questions than the mother. This incident suggests the value of having someone at the assessment meetings who can make sure that the parent understands what is going on, has a chance to question, criticize, and contribute to the planning.

In another instance (also in system C) a school social worker assumes the role of advocate on behalf of the parents at the core evaluation meeting. The father is an unemployed laborer; the mother is also unemployed. Neither has had any formal education beyond tenth grade. After having been told that their child needed a private school placement because of the severity of his learning disability problem, the father said:

He is not much of a problem at home. He seems witty enough. He reads commercials on TV okay.

The psychologist replied: "The problem is between processes. Visual-sequential is not bad. . . ."

There follows a protracted discussion between the psychologist and speech therapist about specific tests.

At this point the school social worker intervenes: "Could you please explain what you mean?"

The psychologist explains the tests in somewhat simpler language.

The speech therapist then remarks: "The visual is really better than the auditory."

The social worker again intervenes: "Sometimes we use terms that we as professionals may know, but others may not."

The speech therapist then explains what "auditory problems" means.

As a result of the intervention of the social worker, the tenor of the meeting has changed substantially, from an esoteric exchange of test scores and descriptions of symptoms to a more informal discussion in which the parents can and do participate. From that point everyone seems to be making a genuine effort to translate concepts into language that the parents can understand. While it was not entirely successful, it did result in a vast improvement in communications during the meeting. Thus the designation of an official child advocate, perhaps even a school employee, could sensitize professionals to problems in making themselves understood. However, in subsequent evaluation meetings the same psychologist immediately lapsed into technical jargon.

Both Chapter 766 and PL 94–142 implicitly assume that the parent is there to represent the child and can, in a sense, serve as the child's advocate in the assessment proceedings. While this may frequently be true, the parent also has needs that may clash with the interests of the child. The Massachusetts law and regulations require that the child be present if over age sixteen or where otherwise appropriate. PL 94–142 also requires that the child attend IEP meetings "where appropriate." Neither state nor federal law recognizes a possible conflict of interest between parent and child. Yet parents may be reluctant to ask questions, to challenge the authority of the school or of the professionals whom they confront in the assessment meetings. Parents may also feel a need to deflect the blame for whatever problems the child is presenting to the school. In the extreme the parents could collude with school officials to secure removal of an unwanted child from the home and community. Such a case, *Bartley* v. *Kremens,* has been brought before the U.S. Supreme Court.

A federal district court in Philadelphia ruled in 1975 that a child cannot be committed to a mental hospital or residential treatment center without being afforded full due process rights, independent of those of the parents. The child, according to the court ruling, has the right to prior notice of hearings and to representation by separate counsel. The American Psychological Association in an amicus curiae brief contended that screening by physicians often reflects the parents' and family's interests more than those of the child.

The physicians' decision is heavily influenced by the parents' attitude toward the child . . . and in instances such as the Bartley case the physician plays the role of family or parental consultant.[13]

The Threatening Parent

Parents are not entirely without resources in the give-and-take that occurs between school and family. Ever present in the assessment deliberations is the possibility, although it rarely occurs, that a parent may not go along with the educational plan and may appeal the school's decisions. There was a widespread belief during the first year that appeals taken by parents would generally be decided in favor of the parents and against the schools. This belief was not the case, but it was nonetheless widely held by school officials. School officials also believed that they would be at a disadvantage in appeal proceedings. The schools could not initiate appeals, but they were in the defensive position of having to answer appeals brought by parents. School personnel feared that they would be without legal counsel in appeal hearings and that parents would generally be represented by counsel or advocacy groups. There was also concern about legal liability for decisions taken in the assessment process— that individual staff members might be sued by parents—although no suits had been brought.[14]

Short of an appeal or threat of appeal, parents could "cause trouble." Causing trouble meant simply being noncompliant or aggressive in questioning school actions. Parents could demand the time and attention of school officials to answer their questions, appear at school committee meetings to question and criticize, or become active in advocacy groups. In system B there was a general concern that failure to adhere to the letter of the law and regulations could result in complaints by parent groups to the politically sensitive school committee. In system A, however, the concern was more about individual parents. System A, serving a more affluent community, has a number of professional and wealthy parents. Such parents represent a threat to the status of school officials; staff members complained that some parents tended to "look down on" them.

Parents who presented such a threat tended to be treated more carefully than others. This treatment is exemplified in the case of Michael P. His mother claimed to have requested an evaluation that was to have been scheduled in the fall of 1974 but never took place. The mother, noting the failure of the school to provide the evaluation, removed the child and placed him in a private school. She was now asking that the school committee pay the private school tuition. School officials wished to avoid paying the tuition and believed the child's needs could be met within the public school. The meeting described here took place toward the end of the school year. It was a strategy session preceding a meeting with the mother. She was described as "an anxious lady, very attractive," who had come to an earlier meeting "wearing what must have been a five-hundred-dollar suit."

There is an unusual concern for observing protocol in dealing with the mother. One official says, for example, "We've got to let her know about the time of the meeting well in advance." Another asks whether she is going to bring her lawyer.

A member of the assessment team: She's going to insist that he is a special-needs child who's been overlooked by the school. She claims to have told the social worker that the child has a learning disability and is suffering from adjustment problems. She claims that she received promises of special services and also claims that she told the same story to the guidance counselor.
Social worker: She puts people on the defensive.
Principal: I won't accept that it was our fault. We don't know when the core was requested. We don't have any letter from her.
Guidance counselor: If we accept that we were wrong, would that hurt the town's position in the final analysis?
Administrator: We could tell them that the kid needed services and we gave them before we did the core. If it is obvious that the kid

needs services, we frequently do it prior to the core. . . . Some towns were behind because they were unable to do all the cores.
Principal: Let's say we had trouble making an appointment with the special consultant and child and let it go from there.
Social worker: I guess she would say, "I'll see you in court."

In another instance a school official told of a parent who had complained at a school committee meeting that the school would not do anything for her child. The official figured that more than one hundred professional hours had been devoted to the family situation.

The school system is paying $15,000 now for private school tuition, and the mother complains that the child got hit in a taxi by another kid. I feel like I worked real hard and got kicked in the teeth for it. After that school board meeting we got a memo from the superintendent asking what we could do about recreation weekends and so forth for the child—and we are already spending $15,000 a year.

School officials sometimes avoid recommendations that might evoke resistance from parents. In the following situation a psychologist backs away from recommending to parents that their child be referred for a psychiatric evaluation, despite compelling evidence of severe emotional problems. The parents, a young articulate professional couple, were themselves divided on the subject. The issue had been presented somewhat obliquely by the psychologist, who then dropped it. It was presented again by the principal:

The problem is not academic, but the other concerns are getting in the way of academics; therefore, one should work with her in getting her feeling better about herself.

At this point, the psychologist again intervenes, changing the subject.

However, the mother comes back to it, asking, "Are you saying that there are emotional problems and it's not intelligence?"

Adjustment counselor (referring to the child's bizarre behavior): The two go together. How do you feel? Have you been comfortable with it?
Mother: No.
Father: I felt it would work itself out.
Mother: Not me. . . .

The psychologist in this instance wished to avoid a possible disagreement with the father even though, as she later told the observer, she was convinced that the child had very serious emotional problems that needed immediate attention.

Orenstein also found striking differences in the ways parents were perceived by school officials in the affluent "Highview" and blue-collar "Bridgeport" schools. One Highview official observed, "Highview parents are as bad as you've heard." Another complained, "It's very difficult to get Highview parents to accept that our judgments are professional judgments. It's not unusual to be halfway through the evaluation of a child and find that his parents have placed him in a day school on their own, and are now expecting us to pay for it." Orenstein reports that Highview school officials feel "under intense pressure from parents: during classroom conferences, teachers experience pressure to recommend children for core evaluation; special educators receive demands for more individual instruction for a particular child; core teams are asked to recommend more services, and particularly, to recommend outside placements." In contrast a Bridgeport official says that parents there "are pretty passive and appreciate whatever the school does for them."[15]

The Absent Parent

The Chapter 766 regulations require that parents have an opportunity before the evaluation to meet with the chairperson of the core evaluation team to discuss the reasons for referral and the nature of the assessments to be performed.[16] The parent is designated a member of the core evaluation team which "shall meet to write the educational plan" for the child and "has the right to be present at and participate in all meetings of the CET [the core evaluation team] where the educational plan is being developed and written. . . ."[17] Of thirty-two observed core evaluations at which the parent's presence was required by regulation, six were conducted and decisions taken in the parent's absence. (On the other hand, at several precore assessment meetings the parent's presence was not required by regulation, but parents were invited and attended because the school officials believed that the parents could contribute to the meetings.)

The Massachusetts regulations provided that where efforts to obtain the parent's presence failed, the matter was to be referred to the regional office of the Division of Special Education, where additional attempts were to be made to get the parents to attend.[18] At the time the observations were made, it was apparent that this procedure was not functioning at all. Referrals made to the regional offices were not being processed. The regional offices had even fewer staff resources than the schools to contact parents and encourage their attendance. As a result, where school officials felt there was a need to provide a service or alter a program in a way that legally could be done only following a core evaluation, the evaluation would proceed without the parent.

Rescheduling a meeting can be a time-consuming, costly, and complicated undertaking since most participants operate on tight schedules with their time committed well in advance.[19] By failing to appear, the parents appear to school personnel to be "bad parents" who do not care about their children. However, their absence may be welcomed, particularly if the parents are considered potentially troublesome. In one meeting a psychologist observed, "I'm glad the parents aren't here since they won't understand what we'll do." The decision at that meeting was to place the child in a special class.

The parent's absence also permits school officials to discuss parents in uncomplimentary terms, often identifying them as the source of the child's problem. For example, a specialist asks: "What about the parents—is it a garden variety genetics?"

Social worker: There is a deceptive quality about the mother. The appearances are okay, but there is a history of depression, although the father is functioning and working hard.
Teacher: She [the child] never talks about her mother—the normal mother relationship seems to be missing.
Principal: I have the feeling, and I don't know from where, that the father is a graduate of a special class here in town.

There follows a discussion of whether the family came from the town or from elsewhere (a particularly salient issue in New England towns) and speculation about the nationality of the family. The teacher then inquires, "What do you suggest if the parents don't accept the special class placement?"

Administrator: I think we don't want to say "special class"; it is really a learning center with a small group that'll be integrated for anything she can handle.

Later in the meeting the principal asks, "Who is going to tell the parents?" She points around the room saying, "Eeny, meeny, miny, mo."

Social worker (who is designated to talk to the parents): Our number one choice is the resource room [special class] with integration. What about the counseling?
Principal: You may not want to hit the mother with both the resource room and the counseling.
Administrator: If she turns down the recommendations, but doesn't want the core—if we recommend the resource room, she can go the hearing route.

The Good Parent

In contrast to the troublesome parent who threatens to disrupt the orderly flow of work by complaining or rejecting recommendations or whose status poses a threat, the good parent is one who goes along. For example, one administrator prior to an education plan meeting said, "Robert has nice parents who are very relaxed and go along with everything. They are the kind of parents you can count on." This assessment was borne out by the quality of participation by the parents in the meeting that followed. The father, a professional person, had little to say. The mother talked about the child's adjustment at home, and both were generally complimentary of the school's efforts in working with the child.

Another woman described as a good parent served as a member of the system's special education parent advisory group. She told the investigator that the group had discussed Chapter 766 but "on an issue-by-issue basis"; their concern was "not in the nature of raising any complaints." She went on to say how happy she was with the services provided and praised the personnel with whom she had come in contact.

School personnel dispense several kinds of reward to the good, compliant parent. The direct approach is to tell the parent what a great job he or she is doing with the child. Consider the following.

Principal: We pointed out what a good job you are doing at home, but you also need our support from here at school.

Later in the meeting the suggestion is made that the child be checked by an ophthalmologist.

The mother: I'll follow through.
Principal: Just like you do about everything else.

The principal continues throughout the meeting to praise the mother for following through on school recommendations.

Good parents were also observed in several instances to have been rewarded by a very subtle instruction to fill out CETA applications so that they would reflect financial need. This reward would occur when a teenage child might be eligible for a part-time CETA position in the school's vocational program. The child's eligibility for the paid position was based on financial need as reflected in information submitted by the parent on the form. In those instances observed the parent would be handed the form with the explanation that eligibility is based on the financial information shown on the form. The parent would be told, "I am sure that your child will be eligible."

When the child's special education needs were relatively clear-cut—where the child was labeled retarded or there was a clear physical disability such as blindness or hearing loss—and where the parents raised no questions about school procedures or services, the child would be described in positive terms. For example:

Candy is just like a flower, just blossoming. It has been a pleasure to work with someone like her who is doing so well.

All the records indicate that he does much better than his test scores would indicate.

He is really a good fellow. I can send him on errands and he is always agreeable.

He is well liked in the community. He is not a fresh kid. And he doesn't talk back.

Assigning Blame

A prominent feature of the assessment meeting is often the assignment of blame, particularly when the cause of the child's difficulty is viewed as somewhat problematic, as in the case of disruptive behavior or learning problems that cannot be attributed directly to intellectual deficits or physical disability. For children who are labeled retarded, the question of causation or blame is rarely at issue in the assessment meetings.

The concern with the assignment of blame is not surprising, given the reliance on a medical or individual deficit model of assessment. Such an approach focuses attention almost exclusively on the child and encourages a search for the "cause" of his or her problem in an examination of the child's history. The solution then depends on application of the appropriate "treatment." What is overlooked is the child's interaction with the larger system, the school, family, and community, which from an ecological perspective may partly explain the child's difficulties. An ecological approach might lead to an examination of the school's structure, personnel, and curriculum and their contribution to the child's problem. However, organizational change is less congenial to school officials than individual change;[20] an "individual deficit" model is preferred, even though this perspective may foster an atmosphere of "blaming the victim."[21]

The regulations governing the core evaluation meeting call for assessments to deal equally with the child's capacities and strengths as well as with deficiencies. That a child is being assessed is in itself a result of someone's concern about a child's deficiencies. The assessment provides official certification that the child has "special needs" that require services in addition to those available to most other children. In other words, if the child is there to be assessed, there must be something wrong with him or her. Much of the core evaluation deliberations are devoted to establishing a pattern of negative functioning of the child through the recitation of test scores, anecdotal information, and observations.[22]

In the following example a report is given on a child who has just been moved to a new school because of disruptive behavior. The guidance counselor, referring to the child's file, reports to the other team members as follows.

Guidance counselor: Most teachers feel it's not enough to give him a grade if he doesn't do much of anything. For example, in social studies he cuts classes. The English teacher reports, "No work." Math, again, "No assignment, no test, he is occasionally disruptive and tries to impress his classmates by being an attention-getter." In science, again the same pattern: "Generally quite disruptive when reprimanded, he acts as if he doesn't know where he is."
Learning disabilities tutor: I can just reiterate this: I have little op-

portunity to tutor him. He doesn't seem to want to be tutored. He comes in order to be a nuisance factor and doesn't want tutoring; he will just slip out.
School adjustment counselor: We have just read about all the weaknesses, but we haven't talked about his strengths.
Learning disabilities tutor: We haven't seen any.

The teacher has a major stake in the assignment of blame. The referral of a child for an evaluation, particularly by someone other than the teacher, is often viewed as an accusation that the teacher has failed to correct or perhaps identify the problem. The teacher then enters the assessment proceedings on the defensive and may seek to blame the parent or child for the child's difficulty.

Assignment of blame may also be used as a bargaining chit. Good parents—those viewed by school personnel as compliant, accepting whatever the school officials wish to do—are rewarded by being absolved from blame for their child's difficulties; those seen as sources of trouble for the school are held responsible for the child's problem, although this is more likely to be discussed in the parents' absence.

The following example illustrates how negative data about the child are used to convince a parent to accept a plan that the parent is expected to oppose. Team members wished to keep the child in second grade. The mother had refused to accept retention of the child in first grade the previous year. The mother is an unmarried black woman on public assistance. (The team members are white.) She is accompanied by her mother. First the child's mother is confronted with the problem.

Psychologist: Her Bender-Gestalt shows her two years below others in her room. She is capable, but she is not learning. She has problems when she has to look and reproduce something that she sees. It takes her longer.
Mother: What can we do?
Psychologist: I have observed her in class many times, and she doesn't feel comfortable there. I found that while she is going into the third grade next year, she is one and a half years behind others in her class, and she is unable to keep up with those in the room. There are new materials presented, and it is no wonder that she feels uncomfortable.

There is further presentation of the child's problem and a description of her as "dyslexic." Then the grandmother suggests that the difficulty might be with the school program rather than with the child.

Grandmother: The basic problem is that she needs much more attention. She needs to be in a smaller class. Sometimes you can go faster in a smaller class.

Her statement is ignored.

Mother (expressing bewilderment): She was smart when she was little.

The teacher adds her essentially negative assessment of the child, followed by the learning disabilities specialist:

The visual attention span and objects went well with pictures, but she couldn't do it with letters. She copies designs at a five-year level and couldn't do the second-grade test. She got thirty-nine mistakes on the first-grade test. It's a learning disabilities problem. Pressure on her is great and she is doing worse now.
Psychologist: We basically came up with the same findings—she is operating at a first-grade level.
Teacher: She's immature and becoming more so. She cries at the drop of a hat. This morning she did an assignment perfectly, and I praised her and she cried. She does not like getting help from peers. I have them pair up in class, but she won't have this at all. She sucks on her clothes sometimes.

The teacher continues with negative examples of the child's behavior. As if this were not sufficient to sell the parent on the proposed retention, science is again invoked for the coup de grace.

Teacher: Earlier in the year, we gave her criteria reference testing, the one with the IBM cards, and she scored grade one plus two months. She was 1.3 years behind at that point.

The teacher then pulls out a computer printout with the child's name on it, presumably showing a listing of skills in which the child is deficient. Finally comes the hard sell.

Psychologist: Alice is now in the second grade and one and a half years below grade level. [Turning to the teacher] What do you see will happen?
Teacher: The gap will be bigger in the third grade. She is a nice, polite girl who has been very unhappy, and I don't want to see her become a discipline problem.
Psychologist: She says she can't do it. Soon we will get to the point where she will say she won't do it.
Learning disabilities specialist: She is there now.

There follow more comments about the child's problem. Then the psychologist asks, "What about services?"

Learning disabilities specialist: She could repeat. But [turning to the psychologist] how about the resource room?
The psychologist explains about the resource room but adds: I don't favor it because it's at another school and I'm not sure that I would recommend moving her at this time; maybe next year we can look at it again. She has a lot of friends here, and if she stays and feels comfortable, would you [turning to the mother] go along with the retention?
Mother: What? Could you repeat that?

The psychologist explains, and the sale is completed.

Mother: Yes, certainly, I do go along. Last year, they didn't want her in the second grade and I insisted. I had to sign a paper, but I decided I wouldn't push it if she can't make it okay.
Psychologist: Last year you could allow catch-up time, but not this year.

Finally, the sale having been completed, the mother is rewarded with a positive comment about the child.

Psychologist: She is really a delightful child, relates well with adults, and I really enjoyed my time with her. I will write this up, send it in the mail, and you take time to read it, sign it, and send it back.

Factors Inhibiting Parent Participation

While the Massachusetts and federal regulations require the participation of parents in team deliberations, they say nothing of the *quality* of participation or how it is to be achieved. Participation can mean an active role in providing information about the child's history and adjustment at home and in the community and in weighing the relative merits of service alternatives. Or it can mean a passive presence and acceptance of decisions taken by school officials. While both extremes were observed, the latter response was by far the more common one. The setting and structure of the meetings, the composition of the evaluation teams, the use of test scores and technical language, together produce enormous pressures for parent acquiescence.

School officials participating in education program planning meetings are under pressure to minimize parent participation. From their perspective, team members, unlike most parents, have the professional qualifications to make judgments about the best plan for the child. This professional training and role permit them to speak with some authority. To the degree that nonprofessionals are permitted to influence professional judgment, the authority of the professional is in danger of being eroded. In a more general sense school officials share a concern for maintaining the predictability of the work setting against intrusions from outsiders, whether they are parents, representatives of advocacy groups, or even school board members. In the case of Chapter 766 the educational plan represents a commitment of resources on the part of the local school system. It may involve sums of money as large as $10,000 to $15,000 per year per child, as ✓ is the case when private school placement is at issue. Financial considerations are in the minds of school officials participating in the evaluations, at least as far as their statements indicate.[23]

In addition to maintaining the authority of the school vis-à-vis the parent and maximizing the predictability of the organizational work setting, school officials also save time by discouraging active involvement and participation in CET deliberations. In the first year of Chapter 766 implementation, all three school systems had far more assessments to complete than they were able to do, and the active encouragement of parent participation took much more time, slowing down the processing of children. This is illustrated by the experience of system C. Of the three systems studied, system C performed markedly better in terms of involving parents in team planning because participation was stressed by the director of special education. Most of the assessment meetings observed in system C were characterized by much give-and-take among all participants, with parents encouraged to participate on an equal footing. There was a great deal of spontaneity about these meetings as evidenced by occasional disagreement among the school professionals present and the soliciting of information and opinion from parents. However, system C had the longest meetings of the three, with more professional staff in attendance. The average time of the meetings observed was 74 minutes, in contrast with 50 minutes in system B and 42 minutes in system A. The average number of participants was 9.5 in system C, as contrasted with 5.7 in B and 6.0 in A.

The qualitatively superior effort exhibited by system C was not without cost. System C completed the fewest evaluations relative to enrollment (2.8 percent versus 3.8 percent in system A and 5.5 percent in system B). This comparison illustrates the trade-off between quality and quantity which, given overwhelming demand and limited resources, was a pervasive feature of all local implementation activities.

PL 94-142 provides financial incentives for local education agencies to locate and assess as many children requiring special needs as possible. State and local entitlements are based on the number of children processed. But there are no incentives for providing services of high quality, and entitlements are too low to pay for all those services required by children who need special education. In other words, the federal law encourages a response that stresses quantity over quality.

Thus pressures to conserve resources and maintain predictability and control of the work environment contribute to a diminution of the parent's planning role, the ascendancy of those who administer and interpret tests, and the channeling of children into predetermined service categories. The following chapter continues the analysis of the core evaluation process with an examination of other means employed by school personnel to manage an overwhelming work load.

5
Individual Treatment and Mass Processing:
The Dilemma of the Street-Level Bureaucrat

Chapter 766 and PL 94–142 are individualizing laws. They provide that each eligible child be assessed individually and that a unique plan be developed and administered to meet the child's special needs. As Massachusetts school personnel at all levels said again and again, poignantly expressing the street-level bureaucrat's central dilemma, "This is the way it should be for *all* children, not just those with special needs." Yet as much as there might be agreement on the desirability of an individualized approach, the reality of mass education forces compromises with this ideal.[1]

The dilemma between individualization and mass processing is shared by street-level bureaucrats in many different human service settings, including public hospitals and clinics, mental health centers, lower courts, public welfare, probation, and employment service offices. Common to these settings is the need to make determinations of eligibility and assessments of service needs that reflect the unique circumstances of individual clients while simultaneously accommodating a case load usually too large to permit sufficient time for each individual case. Working harder or faster or longer hours may help, but only to a point. Other means must be found to cope with service demands that exceed resources.

The training of the semiprofessional and sometimes professional personnel who occupy front-line positions in these bureaucracies, to the extent they are trained at all, is directed toward imparting skills to help individual clients. Nurses, lawyers, social workers, psychologists, doctors, and teachers learn to treat individuals and sometimes families. They are rarely taught skills in case load and work load management, consultation and interdisciplinary collaboration, client advocacy, or organizational change, even though, depending on the specific occupational group to which they belong, many or most will work in large public bureaucracies. On the job, through socialization by colleagues or by their own invention, they learn and apply various means of coping with demands from clients for their services and demands from bureaucratic superiors for completion of the attendant paperwork needed to maintain accountability. They find ways to ration access to service, routinize and ration service provision, standardize and limit service options, and categorize and sort clients to facilitate their processing by the bureaucracy. They also take steps to protect their work environment from unwanted intrusion by clients, or client representatives, or other "outsiders." They do so, however, at some sacrifice to the ideal of individualized treatment espoused in the mission of the organizations that employ them and learned in their formal training.

This chapter continues the analysis of the street-level response to special education reform by examining some of the solutions worked out by school personnel seeking to accommodate excessive work loads. Massachusetts schools were under considerable pressure to complete individualized education programs on all potentially eligible children as quickly as possible, and this pressure contributed to the routinization of the core evaluation meetings. However, all three school systems made some effort to distinguish informally between the more "routine" cases that could be handled with dispatch and the complex cases that required more deliberation. The latter included cases in which one or more team members had a special interest in the child, there was some disagreement among school officials or the outcome was considered problematic, the service plan was likely to be costly, parental opposition was anticipated, or other agencies were involved. In all three systems the complex cases were in the minority.

This informal triage between routine and complex cases provided a way to set priorities on the school's response and thereby conserve staff resources. It allowed school personnel to intervene in a limited number of cases with an individualized approach, consistent with their training and professional self-image. They could then maintain some pride in the quality of their services while at the same time routinizing their responses to most children. A number of school psychologists, for example, insisted on continuing to provide individual counseling to one or two children in order to "maintain their skills," even though their work assignments required full-time testing and participation in evaluation meetings. Such exceptional cases also serve to maintain the image of the bureaucracy as flexible and humanistic in its treatment of clients, even though the majority of cases would not bear this out.

Some front-line school personnel react defensively when it is suggested that special attention be given to children with special needs. For example, in one precore assessment meeting the school adjustment counselor reports the mother's objection to the child's having been tutored by other children in the class. The classroom teacher interjects testily: "I have twenty-one. I just can't get to everyone who needs help. When the quicker ones finish, I help them to help the slower ones."

In another meeting team members are arguing for an individually tailored recreation program for a child whose mother has removed him from the school and is attempting to have the town pay the private school bill. Provision of the recreation program is considered essential to support the town's position that the child's needs can be met within the public school. However, the assistant principal of the high school is none too eager to have the child back. He says, "How is he different from fifteen hundred kids? He doesn't need special recreation programs; he has to accept what's available."

More often, special education staff express frustration at their inability to provide the kind of individualized response to children required by the law and by their own professional commitment. For example, a core evaluation team chairperson recommends to the parents that their seventh grader be placed in a full-time residential school for treatment of his behavior problems. The father asks, "How long will he be there? What about weekends?"

Mother: Wealthy people never have anything to do with their kids; they send them off.
Father: I tell him, don't do anything or they will send you to reform school.

The mother burst into tears at this point. Following the meeting an administrator observes:

The problem is not with the child, but with the school. This is a school failure. We need to individualize to meet the needs of children like this, but we just don't have the resources.

A gifted but disturbed sixteen-year-old high school student expresses to evaluation team members her frustration with negotiating with an impersonal educational bureaucracy:

I'm tired of learning the same things over and over. . . . I don't like the teacher if the teacher doesn't know what he's talking about and a lot of teachers are like that. Classes here are too big, and there are too many kids who don't want to learn. I don't want to be in school, but since I am here I want to learn.

The core evaluation teams sometimes make heroic efforts to circumvent bureaucratic rigidities in designing programs to meet an individual child's needs. This was particularly evident in system C. For example, in the instance of this high school student, the core evaluation team considered a range of alternatives from a private school placement to arranging additional courses at a neighboring university. The outcome was a recommendation to promote the student from the tenth to the twelfth grade, to arrange for summer school programs at a neighboring university (at school committee expense), to select courses taught by individuals with whom it was felt the student could get along, and to provide psychotherapy, also at school expense. There was a sense of adventure among participants as they constructed a program that deviated in so many respects from the normal high school routine. The team chairman, noting that special approval would have to be obtained for the student to make up lost credits, said, "We'll just have to see how flexible or inflexible the school administration is."

A junior high school student, also in system C, was referred for evaluation after having allegedly threatened one teacher and taken a swing at another in the school cafeteria. A number of teachers were reported to be afraid of him. The question was raised about school policy in instances where the child might constitute a danger to others. A psychologist asks, "What is the policy if you have concerns with regard to safety?"

Assistant principal: None. You cannot put a kid out except to the superintendent's office in extraordinary circumstances with a plan for home tutoring; but this is done only for physical injury cases.
Core evaluation team chairman: We need to try everything within the school first before we start talking about putting him out.

(In contrast, the director of pupil personnel services in another system told a parent that their child would be excluded from school unless the parent accepted the proposed educational plan.)

One teacher in the meeting felt that this child needed kindness and firmness and that the proper strategy would be to get him away from some of the stricter teachers. In the ensuing discussion there was frank recognition that some teachers might have provoked or contributed to the confrontations. The psychologist pointed out that the ninth-grade class schedules were arranged by computer, and she wondered whether it weren't possible to do more individual programming to avoid putting the child in classes where he might have conflicts with teachers.

There were numerous examples in system C of efforts to bend rules in order to accommodate to the needs of a child. This frequently involved what they termed a "hand-picked" as contrasted with the normal computer-picked schedule for junior high and high school students. That there might be a problem with specific teachers, however, was never acknowledged to parents. The candid discussions of matching students to the more congenial teachers always took place in precore assessment meetings where the parent was not present. In front of parents school officials invariably sustained the myth that all teachers are equally proficient, interested, and concerned about children.

All three school systems had more or less formal transitional programs to acquaint special-needs children with the large, impersonal, factorylike high school and to enable them to find their way around. In one of the school systems there was a special education vocational counselor. The presence on the staff of someone having official responsibility for assisting the vocational preparation of special-needs youngsters did much in the way of insuring flexible programming, at least for those in special classes at the high school level.

Use of Labels

Earlier I discussed how the use of technical terminology in assessment meetings limits the participation of parents and others unfamiliar with such language. Another form of technical language, diagnostic labeling, was to have been discontinued as a result of Chapter 766. The rationale is stated in the regulations as follows:

The General Court further finds that past methods of labeling and defining the needs of children have had a stigmatizing effect and have caused special education programs to be overly narrow and rigid, both in their content and in their inclusion and exclusion policies.[2]

Yet classroom teachers and specialists were educated in an era when diagnosis meant the assignment of the proper label, which in turn provided the basis for assignment to a special education class or special service. Such terminology is not easily unlearned, as shown in the following examples:

John's speech and behavior is worse. He is more hyperactive. It can be traced to poor interaction in the environment.

He doesn't have the reasoning ability, and in terms of developmental disability, he is borderline; one might term him socially disabled.

The psychologist in a precore assessment meeting tells the special class teacher:

The Bender showed her to have an equivalent score of a five-year-old. However, I don't think she is a trainable, but we might want to consider this to be a trial placement in case the girl seems to need additional help.

At the end of the meeting the special class teacher advises the observer that she runs a program for what were formerly termed "EMH" (educable mentally handicapped) girls.[3] They are now called "substantially independent," she explains.

Here the core evaluation team chairperson tells other specialists:

Sam was getting an awful lot of special help. He used to be, with an IQ under fifty, according to state law, in a trainable class, but he has been in an educable class and had been progressing beyond what one would expect based on test scores alone.

A specialist adds: There is a trainable at Bryant that really turned him off. He is more skilled than that.

In another meeting, a psychologist announces: With regard to the psychological report, I don't have too much. I didn't test him academically. Dorothy, what do you have?

Teacher: He is obviously on the educable-trainable borderline.

In response to a discussion between a psychologist and counselor contrasting programs for "LD kids" and "our kids," the observer asks, "Who are 'our kids?' " The psychologist replies, "Oh, they used to be called retarded."

The director of one special program boasted that anyone examining the records of children in his program would be unable to determine how those children had previously been labeled. However, when asked what kinds of children he had in the program, the director replied, "We have four EMRs, and three EDs, ..."

Fragmentation of Service Delivery

One means commonly employed by street-level bureaucrats to conserve decision-making time is slotting—the classification of clients into either informal or officially recognized categories. Labeling is a form of slotting. Slotting eliminates the necessity to devise individual plans on a case-by-case basis, thereby reducing decision costs.

The processing of children under Chapter 766 may be viewed as a series of slotting decisions.[4] Should a child be referred for an evaluation or not? If referred, which assessments should be performed? Does the child have special needs or not? Into which program prototype should the child be assigned? Which special services should he or she receive? The regulations require the core evaluation team to produce an educational plan for each child that is designed around the child's unique capabilities and limitations. The intent is to fit the services to the child rather than to simply assign the child to existing services. The development of such a plan does not lend itself to slotting decisions. However, team members, faced with the need to make quick decisions, are likely to rely on cues that have worked for them in the past—test scores, labels, and opinions of dominant or "superordinate" professionals.[5] They are also more likely to allocate service by slotting children into existing service categories than to design one integrated plan, uniquely tailored to the child, that might require developing or purchasing new services. Such flexible programming was sometimes carried out in cases regarded by school systems as deserving special attention. However, for the more routine evaluations that make up the bulk of those performed, the core evaluations serve to formalize the routing of the child to existing specialists or programs, each dealing with a single aspect of the child. Instead of specifying learning objectives and how they might be reached, educational plans too frequently resembled the itinerary for a whirlwind tour of school facilities.

A typical child might be referred to the learning disabilities specialist three times per week, the resource room one hour per day five times per week, and to the school adjustment counselor once per week. There could, in addition, be sessions with the remedial reading specialist (for which referral from a core evaluation team was not required), as well as sessions with the speech tutor and special recreation services. (In system C, again an exception, the fragmentation of a child's school week was a concern explicitly raised and taken into account when several different services were contemplated.)

Individual specialists did develop detailed plans for each child describing service goals and how they might be achieved. In systems B and C such written plans were carefully reviewed by service supervisors, thereby assuring that service descriptions met minimum standards of quality and appropriateness, but also adding to the paperwork. The net result was still a fragmentation of the child's day, the addition of new adults to whom the child had to relate, and a diffusion of responsibility for treating the whole child. The classroom teacher who in theory could serve as the coordinator and integrator of services could and frequently did look on the child's learning and adjustment problems as the responsibility of specialists.

Another kind of fragmentation involved the processing of more than one child from the same family. The evaluation process centered around the needs of the individual child who might be referred. If two children from the same family were referred for evaluation, they would be handled as two separate cases. On several occasions, parents raised some question about other children in the family; since the assessment meeting had to do with only one child, these concerns were usually ignored. For example, after hearing about the results of testing on her child, William, the mother looks up and says, "You know I have another boy, Ricky. He probably has that same problem, but they didn't give him those tests. I thought he was lazy and thoughtless, but he was afraid to go into third grade. He wanted to go back to second." The teacher replied, "There is nothing wrong with going back to second." That ended the discussion.

Rationing of Evaluations

During the period of observation there was evidence of another method to reduce time spent in core evaluation meetings. Some teachers, specialists, and principals simply avoided scheduling core evaluations or referring children for evaluations even when the regulations required them.

Following one core evaluation meeting, the psychologist and school adjustment counselor explained that this had actually been an "accidental core." The child's mother works with the relative of a school adjustment counselor who had suggested that the mother request a core evaluation. When asked whether the evidence had not indeed substantiated the child's need for services, the psychologist replied, "Of course, but without the core evaluation, the parents could have sat down with the teacher, and the psychologist could have come in and observed the child's behavior in the class. We then could have dealt with the problem without going through the core evaluation process."

In one system it was common practice for specialists at the individual school level to decide informally whether a child should be referred, based not on the presenting problem but rather the presumed solution. If it was believed that the services of additional specialists would have to be bought, a quick evaluation would be held. (All systems studied had a roster of part-time, hourly-rate specialists for whom payment could be authorized by core evaluation team recommendations.)

In another instance a principal told of efforts to discourage a mother from formally requesting an evaluation of a child. The parent had finally insisted, and the evaluation had been held. Observation of these evaluations suggested that the school officials were indeed reluctantly going through the motions of the evaluation only because the parent had insisted. In the meetings the school officials offered considerable reassurance that the problem would be taken care of within the school and that the parent should not worry so much about it. The implication was clear that the parent's concern was inappropriate. A school adjustment counselor told the parent:

I am not going to pull any punches, I think you are magnifying the problem. Mary mirrors your behavior. She absorbs subconsciously your fears and mother's anxiety that she is not competing with her friends. Parents are bad as tutors. You are putting on the pressure. Try and relax yourself."

The parent was later reassured that she needn't worry about school: "We have excellent people here."

The very real concerns of these parents about dealing with the emotional problems of their children were touched on in a very patronizing way. Parents were simply told not to worry about it.

Failure to Respond to Parent Concerns

Another solution to the ever-present problem of demand in excess of resources was the rationing of services. This rationing took several forms. There was a failure of school officials to respond to concerns raised by parents. There was also an increased reliance on student interns or trainees, a reduction in hours of specialist service per child, and a greater reliance on group instead of individual service provision. Initiation of some types of service was simply deferred.

The failure of team members to respond to concerns of parents was prevalent in evaluations in which a decision had been reached before the meeting with the parent. Any intrusion of additional concerns by the parent was an unwelcome deviation from a fixed agenda. Unless such concerns could be accommodated in the plan that had already been formulated by school officials, they would simply be ignored or deflected to the parent.

In some instances parents expressed a desire for a specific learning content for their child. For example, one parent said that he would like his daughter to learn how to write her name in cursive script so that she could sign for things. He also wished her to learn how to count money and make change. The chairperson assured the parent that this was "a reasonable request" that could easily be taken care of. There were also examples of parents requesting swimming, special woodworking, or recreational programs. When these could be accommodated easily, school officials acquiesced. Situations involving emotional concerns or services that might cost the schools additional funds were more likely to be ignored.

One parent complained at length about disagreements she and her husband were having about parenting practices and their inability to cope with the emotional problems of their five-year-old kindergarten child. The picture that emerged was one of a family in crisis. The parent was told "He [the child] is too young to assign to a school adjustment counselor, but the school adjustment counselor might be available for you to talk to." Whereupon the school adjustment counselor who was present at the meeting stated, "You ought to follow up with counseling at the mental health center."

Mother: I am afraid it costs too much money.
School adjustment counselor: The center has a sliding scale.

At this point the psychologist intervenes and changes the subject, ending the discussion.

This failure to provide help contravenes provisions of the Massachusetts regulations that quite clearly stipulate that the school has a responsibility for providing counseling for parents where indicated as necessary for the child's educational adjustment:

For each school-aged child with special needs, each school committee shall provide or arrange for the provision of the following services to the child or the child's parents—whenever such services are recommended as part of the child's educational plan. . . . Sustained individual casework provided by a social worker to a school-aged child with special needs or the parents of such a child . . . and group sessions conducted within the public school by a psychologist or a psychiatrist for school-aged children with special needs or the parents of such children. . . . Individual consultation by a psychologist or psychiatrist about an identified problem with the school-aged child with special needs or the parents of such a child. Sustained individual treatment intervention provided by a psychologist or psychiatrist to a school-aged child with special needs or the parents of such a child. . . . If a CET finds that a medical, psychological or social service, in addition to those listed in paragraphs 503.1(c) through 503.1(j), should be provided as an essential part of the child's educational plan, and the regional review board approves such a finding, the school committee should provide or arrange for the provision of such services.[6]

Three factors contributed to this tendency to ignore certain kinds of parental concern. First, there was a reluctance to deviate from the plan already worked before the meeting with the parent. One psychologist noted that he had been under considerable pressure from the school principal to reduce the time spent in core evaluation meetings. He had, in fact, succeeded in cutting the duration of assessment meetings, but it appeared that this reduction had been achieved at the expense of any spontaneity or problem solving in these meetings. I observed three meetings conducted by this person. Each had the same contrived, rehearsed quality. Much of the language used to describe problems and treatment alternatives in the three meetings was exactly the same.

Second, team members seemed not to know what to do about reports of emotional problems presented by parents. If the problem of a child was emotional or had an identified emotional component, the solution was generally a referral to the school social worker or adjustment counselor. These staff members seldom had the time to work with the children referred to them in more than a perfunctory way. Problems of a more serious nature were occasionally treated by referral to the school consulting psychiatrist or to an outside agency for evaluation. However, lower-level school officials, specialists, and teachers appeared uncomfortable with presentations of emotional or parenting problems and unfamiliar with requirements that the schools assist with these problems. When asked after assessment meetings why parental pleas for help were overlooked, the response was frequently, "Well, I was hoping the school adjustment counselor would pick up on that." Or, "The school adjustment counselor was not here and that's his [or her] job."

Third, school officials were concerned about costs. While the core evaluation teams were ideally to make their plans free from financial constraints, in reality such constraints played a prominent part in their deliberations. Payment for medical or counseling services for parents or for children outside the school was at this time the subject of some controversy. Several school systems had announced that, regulations and reimbursements notwithstanding, they would not pay the costs of any outside medical or psychological services.

There was some variation among the three school systems with regard to the intrusion of financial concerns in the core evaluation process. In system C, the poorest of the three, there was frequent discussion during the core evaluation meetings of the cost of outside services, including private school placements, psychological, medical, and recreation services. But the prevailing view often expressed by the director of special education was, "If the service is needed, we will fight to get the school committee to pay for it." In system A, where the budget for special education services had been exceeded, there was considerable concern among administrators about limiting costs. Administrators believed that some principals used the core evaluation process to replace services that had been cut from regular budgets. One official confided that a private school placement for a particular child, while indicated, would not be recommended because of the expense. The core evaluation team's position would be that the child's needs could be met within the public school system, although the principal very vocally opposed the return of the child to his school. System A also maintained an unofficial quota for private school placements. They sought to avoid a private placement unless a child already in a private school could be returned to the public school, thereby opening up a slot.

In the following case a mother described by a team chairperson as "slightly retarded" is cajoled into paying for a service that the school system is responsible for providing. The mother receives social security. She is referred to throughout the meeting by her first name and talked to in a somewhat playful, slightly condescending way as one might, for example, treat a particularly precocious four-year-old. The team wishes to enroll the child in a summer program. The teacher states that $75 is needed for the camp plus $135 for transportation.

The public welfare social worker says, "Wilma can pay this. She just received over a thousand dollars retroactive social security. She has plenty of money in the bank." There follows general joking with Wilma about how rich she is.

Team chairperson: The school department won't pay. [To the mother] This is a five-week program, and he will still be home three or four weeks of the summer. It will be worth the $200 for the respite.
Social worker [to the mother]: What about the $35 you won last night in bingo?

The mother's complaints that she doesn't want to spend the money are disregarded amid joking about the mother's "tightness."

Reliance on Student Trainees

There was considerable reliance on unpaid student interns, particularly in system A, for individual and group counseling, recreation, testing, and tutoring services. These students were completing practicum requirements at local universities. It was clear that in addition to meeting a commitment to train personnel, students were being used to provide services that would not otherwise be available. In a number of instances in this same school system, core evaluation team recommendations were made contingent upon the availability of students to carry out a particular type of service. School personnel generally spoke quite highly of the creativity and commitment of students serving internships within the system. However, there were also examples of scapegoating of students. One mother complained about lack of communication with a tutor. All present expressed doubt that this could have been the case, until someone pointed out that the tutor in question was a student. In another instance there was a considerable disparity—twenty points—between the previous year's and the current year's IQ tests. When it was pointed out that last year's test had been administered by a student, all immediately agreed to accept the current test as valid without further question.

Stretching Staff Resources

The most frequent outcome of a core evaluation team meeting was the recommendation that a child be referred to a specialist for services. At the same time, specialists, while carrying a regular case load, were spending more of their time testing, filling out forms, and attending assessment meetings. Therefore, while more referrals for specialist services were being generated, specialists had less time to work with individual children. Some additional personnel were hired, but in no instance was the addition of new staff sufficient to pick up the overload. Interviews with school adjustment counselors, learning disabilities specialists, and tutors suggested that this dilemma was being met in several ways. There was increased reliance on student interns. In addition, most specialists reported that they "worked harder" and were more likely to work at home. This was particularly true of personnel who had responsibilities for preparing reports as part of the assessment process. But most specialists also reported seeing fewer children than before.

Specialists also rationed services by seeing children for shorter periods of time. A learning disabilities specialist who might previously have seen a child individually for four or five half-hour sessions per week might now see the child for three twenty-minute periods. Specialists also saw more children in groups. Some specialists were inclined to rationalize this shift to group treatment as more efficacious. For example, a learning disabilities specialist, saying that she would see a child together with another in twice weekly tutoring sessions, commented, "She needs the experience in sharing my attention with another child." Another specialist remarked, referring to the necessity to provide group treatment instead of one-to-one counseling, "He needs the experience in a small group situation." While no data were available to document the extent of revised practice standards in view of increased case loads, my impression was that this revision was widespread in all three systems.

The Case of Janice B.

By way of summary, I present the following account of one core evaluation meeting that illustrates many of the points raised in this and the preceding chapters. It shows how concerned and committed school personnel, under severe pressure to conserve time while meeting requirements to evaluate and serve children on a mass basis, unintentionally distort provisions for individualized assessment planning and parent involvement.

Janice is nine years old and in the fourth grade. The meeting is chaired by a psychologist. Also present are the learning disabilities specialist, the fourth-grade teacher, and the child's mother, a woman with limited education.

The teacher opens the meeting with a negative assessment of the child.

Teacher: She is below in her fourth-grade subjects, has problems staying in line, following directions, and following what was said in class.

Next, a label is applied.

Psychologist: The doctor examined her and said that Janice should be wearing glasses at all times. We suspected a perceptually handicapped problem.

Following a discussion of the child's vision problem, the psychologist continues with a technical description of test results that the mother cannot understand.

Psychologist: With regard to testing, she has an awful lot of difficulty in the visual-motor area and scored six years, that is, three years below where she is. She understands that she has this difficulty. She does have the potential to learn, an average intelligence. For example, her Peabody test was 104; in her WISC she was below average; and with the performance subtest she sees and does things below average. Academically, the Wide Range Achievement test was substantially below. In reading and math she is at the third grade. In math she is two years below.

The attack continues.

Learning disabilities specialist: I gave the learning disabilities test and found a low auditory attention span below three years. The visual attention span was low, about six years. There are motor problems. Her handwriting is indecipherable and it is all wrong. It is as if she never learned how. When we get her working on her attention span, it will help. She had double the errors on one of the tests and does have the kinds of problems my department would work on.

The discussion continues in this vein with contributions from the psychologist, learning disabilities specialist, and classroom teacher, mostly negative. Finally the psychologist pauses and asks the mother, "Do you have any questions at this point?"

Mother: Why is she having these problems? Is it just now, or has she had it from the beginning?

The discussion now turns to the question of blame. The school personnel are unanimous in their judgment that it is the child's fault. The learning disabilities specialist answers the mother, "It has been from the beginning."

Teacher: I looked at the records from the Meridian school and she has had poor grades. Each year she has been falling further behind. In the fourth grade, they just don't teach third-grade subjects, and in the fifth, they don't teach fourth.
Psychologist: What we have here now is a youngster going into the

fifth grade who is not functioning at the fifth-grade level. We can
discuss what to do.
Mother: Why is she falling behind?
Psychologist: Many things are not understood. There is an inherited
component.

In other words, not only is the child at fault, but the mother is to
blame as well. In addition, the child's problem has been defined as
an inability to fit into the gradations established by the school; if
the child does not conform to the expectations of the fifth-grade
teacher, the child does not belong there. We see here an example of
a school failure, the failure of the school to accommodate to the
needs of this child. School officials, however, make the case that it is
not the school's fault; it is the child's and the parent's.[7]

The mother seems dismayed and relates problems she is having
with her other children. These concerns are ignored. The mother,
perhaps to deflect some of the responsibility from herself, also
engages in child blame. "I think maybe she is not trying as hard. At
one time she says that she can't do it and won't do it."

There follows more discussion of Janice's problem, and her condition is described by the learning disabilities specialist as "dyslex-
ia," a term that no one bothers to explain to the mother. The
psychologist then asks the teacher, "What if she were to go on to
the fifth grade?"

This is a rhetorical question. The psychologist had told the observer before the meeting that the team planned to recommend
retention in the fourth grade.

Teacher: She would feel frustration and would get to feeling worse.
Forcing her into the fifth grade would be bad.
Psychologist: Are we talking about keeping her in the fourth grade?
The mother agrees, saying, "I don't want her to go on."

The discussion then turns to possible inclusion of the child in a
special learning disabilities summer program conducted by the
learning disabilities specialist at the school. The learning disabilities
specialist says she would also like to see Janice during the school
year for thirty minutes per day to work on her auditory and motor
skills. The discussion about retention has a definitely contrived
quality about it as if it had been rehearsed in advance, which, in fact,
it was. At this point, in the context of discussing Janice's attendance
at the summer program, the mother introduces another problem.

Mother: The only problem is that my husband is ill. He has been ill four years now, and this is the first time we can get away. We will have three weeks in July when we will be gone.
Learning disabilities specialist: That's no problem. Summer school will be June 30 to August 15.

Again some information about the family of concern to the mother is nevertheless ignored by the members of the assessment team. The mother has previously said that she has other children with whom she is having problems. Now we learn that her husband has been ill for four years. We later learn that the mother was the last to know of the proposed retention. The learning disabilities specialist describes how she has already prepared Janice for staying in the fourth grade. The teacher adds that she has retained another child who is now doing quite well. The teacher states, "If you have to stay back because you're naughty, that's bad; if you stay back because you can learn more things, then that's fine. That's what I told Janice."

At this point, the psychologist tells the mother that there will be "a home visitor who will come, a woman, and she will discuss these things with you."

It is not clear from the context what things are to be discussed by the home visitor. Furthermore, under Massachusetts regulations, the home visit, conducted by the school adjustment counselor, should have been completed before the assessment. The mother at this point again raises a question about another child, saying, "Maybe we ought to do this [the core evaluation] for William, too."

No one picks up on this. The psychologist then summarizes the educational plan:

There will be three things: first, retention in the fourth grade; secondly, time with Norma [LD specialist] starting in September; and third, a summer program starting on June 30. I will write this up and you will get it, but it will take a long time before you receive it in the mail.

At this point, the mother reports what seems a very appropriate and insightful comment of her child:

Janice says Miss Connor [teacher's name] gave up on me and won't help me.

Everyone laughs.

Miss Connor responds: She's right. I have a rule. I just won't help anyone who won't follow directions. And when she does pay attention, she can't remember.

Again the child is blamed. While the child has, in fact, correctly assessed the situation ("Miss Connor gave up on me"), there is no room for attributing a share of the problem to either the structure of the school ("They don't teach fourth-grade subjects in the fifth grade") or to the unwillingness of the teacher to work with a child whom she obviously does not like ("I just won't help anyone who doesn't follow directions").

Following the meeting, I asked the psychologist why they had recommended retention of a child with a teacher who was obviously not interested in working with her. The psychologist replied that the teacher was leaving at the end of the school year. He agreed that the teacher had stopped working with the child and that this was indeed part of the problem. He added, "We would never have recommended leaving the child with that same teacher." However, none of this was shared with the mother. Members of the assessment team maintained before the mother that the problem was entirely the child's, and they have supported the fiction that all school personnel are uniformly committed and qualified to correct the child's problems.

6
Teachers and Specialists:
Who Is Responsible for the Child?

A very small percentage of children with special needs are served in self-contained special classes.[1] Most spend the greater portion of the school day in regular classes and receive supplementary help from specialists. The regular class teacher, particularly at the elementary level, plays the pivotal role in the school's treatment of children with special needs.

In some respects the situation of the teacher is well suited to this role. The teacher interacts with the same children daily over a ten-month period and can observe and assess each child's learning potential, skills, and behavior, individually and in relation to peers. In recognition of the individual differences among all children, the teacher is granted relative autonomy in the classroom, which permits different interventions with children who have different learning needs. The teacher's task is to take a class of children with varying abilities, learning styles, and personalities, and work toward passing on at the end of the year a cohort with uniform knowledge and skills.[2] However, as a street-level bureaucrat, the teacher must constantly seek a balance between the conflicting demands on his or her time from the group as a whole and from individuals within the group. The need to manage and relate to a large group of children severely restricts individual intervention; time taken with one child is time taken from the group as a whole.

Consequently teachers may seek relief from attending to children who, because of their special needs, demand a greater share of their time. This is particularly true of disruptive children whose behavior commands the attention of the teacher. Educational specialists are potential sources of help to the teacher, but they are at the same time the gatekeepers who determine access to that help. This fact has important implications for the nature of the work relationships between teachers and specialists.

Recognition of the teacher's central role under Chapter 766 is reflected in provisions for teacher referral of children believed to have special needs, for teacher participation in assessment and development of the education plan, and for support services and training for regular class teachers.[3] PL 94–142 regulations have similar provisions relating to the role of regular class teachers. Both PL 94–142 and Chapter 766 require that education for children with special needs be offered in a regular education setting whenever appropriate and feasible; the classroom teacher must of necessity play a decisive role if this mainstreaming strategy is to succeed.

Aside from the procedural requirements of the law and regulations, the classroom teacher appears to have much to gain from the implementation of special education reform. Federal and Massachusetts laws specifically recognize that some children may require services beyond those that may normally be expected from the teacher. It provides sanction for the designation of certain children as "special." This means that the teacher's experience and skills are not expected to suffice in all instances; some children may require additional help.

The law gives teachers an officially sanctioned opportunity to share with others problems in working with specific children and provides a means of obtaining help. The assessment process also offers an occasional chance for the teacher, normally isolated from colleagues, to get out of the classroom and engage with other professionals in joint problem solving.[4] The development of the Individualized Education Program can, at least theoretically, aid the teacher in providing increased accountability, make teacher preparation more relevant, direct attention to specific learning activities, help motivate students to achieve specific objectives, and facilitate cooperation with parents.[5] A summary report of research on IEPs concluded that while there were a number of problems, "findings suggest that once an efficient IEP process is underway, . . . it tends to be instructionally relevant to at least those teachers who favor a diagnostic/prescriptive precision or behavioral approach to teaching."[6]

How in fact was the process perceived and implemented by classroom teachers in Massachusetts? What effect did Chapter 766 have on the way teachers work with children identified as having special needs? What difference did it make for children so identified and evaluated? A prime concern of the study was the impact of the law on its intended beneficiaries, the children designated as having special needs. It was not possible to measure directly the effect that being identified, referred, assessed, and served had on these children without unduly intruding on their lives. I was therefore restricted to measures that enabled me to learn only what others believed or reported. I observed assessment meetings, examined school records, and interviewed those involved in assessment and service provision in three school systems. I also traced the experience of a sample of children to determine the immediate outcome of the assessment and education plan development process as reported by their teachers. This procedure also enabled me to inquire about the teachers' perception of the process and their role in it.

The records of the three school systems revealed considerable variation in the rate of evaluations—the number of evaluations as a percentage of total enrollment—in individual schools. Some schools were performing many more evaluations than others, and discussions with school officials confirmed that the variation did not just reflect a higher incidence of problems in these schools.[7] I decided to follow children in the elementary schools that in March 1975 showed the highest rate of evaluations completed to date. A total of six schools was selected—one in system A, two in system B, and three in system C.

The interviews with teachers in these schools were conducted in May and June; therefore a minimum of three months had elapsed since the development of the education programs for the children who had earlier been identified as having special needs. In most instances a much longer time had passed. In all cases there had been sufficient time for the education program to be implemented.

The Massachusetts regulations require that the education plan set forth a "specific statement of the educational goals which the child can reasonably be expected to achieve during the following three months, six months, nine months. . . ." They also require that a member of the core evaluation team (CET) monitor the child's progress toward reaching these goals and submit "at least quarterly, to the child's parents, to the CET, and the principal" a written report on the child's progress.[8] Given these requirements, it seemed reasonable to expect teachers to have noted the effects of the implementation of the educational plan on the child's learning.

I interviewed the teachers of all the children in the six elementary schools who had been evaluated earlier in the year, according to school records, a total of seventy-nine children.[9] The breakdown by school system is shown in table 3.

Seventy-one percent of the children were in third grade or below; another 6 percent were in ungraded classes, and the remaining

Table 3
Follow-Up Interviews by School System

	Number of Students	Percentage
System A	7	8.8
System B	38	48.1
System C	34	43.1
Total	79	100.0

23 percent were distributed among the fourth through seventh grades. This grade distribution closely resembles that of the total population in system B, but it overrepresents the lower grades in relation to populations evaluated in systems A and C. As a result, the sample is somewhat skewed in the direction of underrepresenting the more complex or "serious" cases and, conversely, overrepresenting the more routine cases identified through screening programs.

Characteristics of Teachers

I interviewed forty-four teachers who had the seventy-nine children in their classes. The teachers interviewed were overwhelmingly female (89 percent) and had considerable teaching experience. Thirty percent had been teaching nine or more years, and only 19 percent for two years or less. The mean number of years taught was 8.4. All had at least a bachelor's degree; 27 percent had a master's degree as well. The average class size was twenty children.

The Role of the Regular Class Teacher

The focus of the interview with teachers was on each child evaluated earlier in the year. The teacher was asked what was now being done to help the child and what the teacher's experience had been with the core evaluation process.

Responses indicated that teachers believe most of the children are receiving more assistance as a result of or following the core evaluations, but they essentially view their own role as peripheral. They see the whole process from referral through assessment and provision of services as belonging to someone else. Contrary to the mainstreaming thrust of the law which aims at integrating the teacher into the special education process, there is considerable reality to this view.

According to the teachers' responses, 67 percent of the children were, as might be expected, receiving less (30.4 percent) or no (36.7 percent) services before the evaluation. Another 20.2 percent of the children were described as having received the same or more (2.5 percent) services before the core evaluation.

While the teachers reported that most of the children were getting more help following the core evaluations, specialists, not teachers, were providing this help. When asked who was providing the services, teachers of 10.3 percent of the children included themselves among those helping the child with the problem identified as the basis for referral. For the remaining 89.7 percent of the children, one or more specialists were designated as providing the necessary services.

The Education Plan

The major product of the core evaluation process is the education plan. According to the Massachusetts regulations, the education plan should set forth general goals as well as more specific behavioral objectives for immediate (next three months) and more distant future. The plan should also describe the specific steps to be taken, methods and materials to be used, and personnel to be working with the child. If the services of specialists are required, the plan is to include a detailed description of what the specialist plans to do and what the outcome is expected to be.[10] The education plan, agreed to by all members of the assessment team, which is to include teachers as well as parents, becomes the design for the education of the child. As such, one expects that the plan would be of major use to the classroom teacher who has the child in class for all or most of the day.

While the regulations stipulate that the teacher currently having the child or who is likely to have the child following evaluation shall be a member of the core evaluation team, not all teachers were actually involved. Teachers reported having participated in the core evaluation meeting for only fifty (63 percent) of the seventy-nine children. They reported having been specifically involved in the development of the education plan for only forty-four (56 percent) of the children. To put it another way, teachers were *not* involved in the development of education plans for 44 percent of the children, nearly half those evaluated.

The school systems in this sample were among the leaders in the state in expenditures for special education and in community wealth and were highly regarded by education professionals for the quality of their programs. Thus nationally the problem of teacher noninvolvement may be of even greater scope than these findings indicate. The noninvolvement of teachers is not simply a reflection of the difficulties encountered in launching a major new program; the Massachusetts Legislature's Special Commission on Chapter 766 found that noninvolvement still is a problem five years after the law was passed and three years after its initial implementation.[11]

The noninvolvement of teachers in education program development has been reported elsewhere. A joint study of 230 planning team conferences by the Connecticut Department of Education and the U.S. Bureau of Education of the Handicapped found:

Special education teachers received more information than regular education teachers prior to the meeting.

Administrators and appraising personnel dominated meetings.

Teachers tended to play passive roles; [they] felt inhibited by the principal's presence and thus [had little] participation.

Most planning team members did not know the full purposes and scope of committee activities. Instructional staff knew less . . . than administrators and support personnel.

Parents [did] not participate actively in decision making.

Decisions [were] made by one or two individuals . . . and not through a group decision-making process.[12]

In this study teachers reported that parents were much more involved in the development of education plans than they themselves had been. Teachers offered information about the extent of parent involvement for 67 of the 79 children. Of these, teachers reported either heavy (10.8 percent) or moderate (75.4 percent) involvement of parents in the development of the education plan. This teacher perception of heavy parent involvement was not supported by my observations of core evaluations at which parents were present but not involved.

A minority of teachers (6, or 13.6 percent) did voice concern that parents were being intimidated by the core evaluation process. Typical complaints were, "Parents are left out," "Parents don't know their rights; schools probably don't want them to," "Teachers feel intimidated by the professionals, and most parents feel threatened by the number of persons present in the core evaluation meetings," "Parents are overpowered. That mother was just scared and defensive."

It is not surprising in view of their lack of involvement that only a minority of teachers considered the education plan useful. Teachers were asked, "Is the education plan a useful guide for providing ways to help [student's name]?" The responses are shown in table 4.

For only about one-third of the 79 students did the teacher give an unqualified yes response. For the remaining two-thirds the teachers gave a negative or mixed response or none at all. Eight of the 44 teachers (18.2 percent) volunteered that they had never seen the education plan. Several of these teachers were not even aware that the children in question had been evaluated and found to have special needs.

A number of teachers commented that the education plan was not specific enough to be useful as a prescription for intervention. Other comments indicated that while some thought the process to

Table 4
Teacher Responses to Question,
"Is the Educational Plan a Useful Guide?"

	Number of Students	Percentage
Yes	26	32.8
No	13	16.5
Mixed	24	30.4
No Response	16	20.3
Total	79	100.0

be worthwhile, they felt the plan itself was of little benefit to them. The following comments are typical:

There is not enough detail for teachers; it's primarily for specialists. The discussion was useful, but I never saw anything in writing.
The teacher knows the least. She refers, but gets nothing new in the way of suggestions. It is a very lonely situation doing it all by yourself.
It is not that specific; there are no academic goals.
It was useful to write it, but not to follow it; someone should have written it who knew the child.

The purpose of the education plan is not solely to prescribe ways in which the classroom teacher is to work with the child. The plan may also describe work to be performed by specialists outside the classroom. Thus classroom teachers may stand to benefit from the core evaluation process in another way. A child referred for evaluation may, if it is recommended by the CET, be sent for part of the day to a specialist or resource room. The process then offers both a means of securing special help for children with whom the classroom teacher is experiencing some difficulty and occasional relief from having that child in class. While there is evidence that resources rooms are used inappropriately to exclude unruly children from regular classes, the "escape valve" function of the core evaluation process did not work to the teachers' satisfaction.[13]

Discrepancy between Teacher Expectations and Results

I wished to learn the teachers' perceptions of the problems presented by the 79 children in the sample and of the kinds of services prescribed in the education plans. For each of the 79 children the teachers were asked, "What kinds of problems affect his or her performance in school?" The responses were coded using the same categories of referral problem appearing on the education plan form.[14] This question was intended to elicit the teachers' own assessments of the problem or problems rather than their knowledge of the "official" reason for referral or the "official" team finding as set forth on the referral and education plan. The teachers' responses are summarized in table 5.

Table 5
Teachers' Report of Children's Problems

	Problem A		Problem B	
	Number of Students	Percentage	Number of Students	Percentage
Learning Disorder	33	41.8	9	11.4
Behavioral or Family Counseling	23	29.1	23	29.1
Other	19	24.1	15	19.0
No Response	4	5.0	32	40.5
Total	79	100.0	79	100.0

The teachers could and in many instances did indicate more than one problem for each child. A learning problem was listed as the first reason (problem A) for 41.8 percent of the children, and a behavioral or family problem was listed as first for 29.1 percent. For the remaining 24.1 percent for whom responses were given, the problems were distributed among hearing, speech, vision, mobility, and other categories, shown as "Other" in table 5. A second problem (problem B) was listed for 47, or approximately 59 percent, of the students. Of these about half were behavior or family problems. Taken together (problem A plus problem B), teachers were concerned with behavior problems of well over half the children—46 of the 79 children, or 58 percent; learning problems were specified for a total of 42 children, or 53 percent. The services provided these children, as reported by their teachers, seldom address behavior or family problems.

The teachers were asked, "What kinds of things are being done to help him or her with these problems?" and "Who is providing these services?" Again the responses were coded according to the categories on the official education plan form. The teacher could name any number of services and specialists for each child. Table 6 shows the number of children reported by teachers to be receiving help from counselors or social workers.

In most Massachusetts schools the specialist responsible for behavior, emotional, or family problems is the school social worker or

Table 6
Teacher Reports of Children Receiving Services from Counselors

	Number of Students	Percentage
Children Seeing School Social Worker or Adjustment Counselor	13	16.5
Outside Counseling	4	5.0
Neither	62	78.5
Total	79	100.0

adjustment counselor. However, only 13 of the 79 students (16 percent) were reported by their teachers to be receiving services from the school social worker or adjustment counselor. An additional 4 children (5 percent) were reported to be receiving counseling outside the school system. Thus, while teachers indicated that well over half the children (58 percent) had behavior or emotional problems affecting their learning, only 21.5 percent were said to be getting any help either outside the school system or from the school specialist responsible for treating such problems.

In contrast, a total of 42 children (53 percent) were reported by teachers as having learning problems. Forty-eight children (61 percent) were reported to be receiving help from the learning disabilities specialist. If we add the number of children receiving help in the resource room (13), the percentage of those receiving help with learning problems is even higher (77 percent). In other words, while most of the special needs children in their classes are perceived by teachers as having behavior problems, relatively few are receiving help for these problems. Most of the services are instead addressed to learning problems that are of less concern to teachers.

Just how accurate are these perceptions? The teachers tended to assign to parents a more prominent role in assessment and education plan development than the facts warranted. Perhaps they underestimated the level of services available for children exhibiting behavior problems. Table 7 shows the total distribution of services planned for children in the three school systems for whom evaluations had been completed.[15]

As table 7 indicates, counseling services represented from about

Table 7
Services Recommended by Core Evaluation Teams*

Service	System A		System B		System C	
	Number	%	Number	%	Number	%
Counseling Services**	60	20.9	100	13.6	181	28.6
Resource Room	46	16.0	98	13.3	78	12.3
Learning Disability Tutor	75	26.0	298	40.5	165	26.1
Speech	19	6.6	142	19.3	39	6.2
All Other Services	87	30.3	98	13.3	169	26.7
Total Services	287	99.8***	36	100.0	632	99.9***

*As shown on the completed educational plan forms. Any child may have from zero to five different services recommended.
**Includes referrals to the school adjustment counselor, guidance counselor, or social worker, ED tutor, or to an out-of-school counseling situation for the child or parents.
***Does not equal 100 percent due to rounding.

14 to 29 percent of all service referrals recommended by the core evaluation teams. (Since a child might have more than one kind of counseling service recommended, the number of children for whom counseling services were designated would be less than the number of referrals shown in table 7.) In contrast, referrals for learning problems varied from 26 to 40 percent; if resource room referrals are added, the total learning referrals are from 38 to 54 percent. These data tend to confirm that there is indeed a discrepancy between teachers' perceptions of the kinds of problem they are concerned about and the responses to these problems by the core evaluation teams, although this discrepancy may vary, depending on the level of services available in a particular school system.

This finding is supported, at least indirectly, by other studies. In one study a behavioral checklist was completed by 2664 Florida regular class teachers, K–12, for all children in their classes. The teachers identified 20.4 percent of the children as exhibiting behavior disorders. For 12.6 percent these disorders were "mild"—the children could be helped in the regular class setting with extra counseling; 5.6 percent were "moderate," and 2.2 percent "severe."[16]

The U.S. Bureau of Education for the Handicapped (BEH) has estima-
ted the prevalence of "emotional disturbance" as only 2 percent of
school-age children.[17] During the 1976–77 school year, 284,385 children. The schools studied were, if anything, far better than most in
the number of such children served and the nature of services designated for them. Nonetheless, the regular class teachers believed
vices, but only about 0.6 percent of all school-age children.[19] Thus
the 2 percent BEH estimate means that only about 30 percent of
"emotionally disturbed" school-age children were being served.
The imprecision of categorical definitions and the rudimentary nature of the reporting by local and state education agencies limits
confidence in these estimates. I mention them only to make the
point that while children with emotional or behavior problems are
of major concern to classroom teachers, special education and related services are directed to a very limited proportion of such children. The schools studied were, if anything, far better than most in
the number of such children served and the nature of services designated for them. Nonetheless, the regular class teachers believed
that such services were insufficient and that the behavior problems
they confronted in their classrooms were not being adequately addressed through current special education service options.

In a 1977 Massachusetts study the assessment information provided by teachers for 165 students was compared with the education plans recommended by the core evaluation teams for these
same students. The investigator found "no meaningful significant
relationships between any of the problem categories [specified by
teachers] and the CET placement decisions." In other words, teacher
assessments bore no observable relation to decisions made by the
evaluation teams even though the teachers were supposed to be
members of these teams. What was related to the assessment outcomes was the IQ test. The author states, "The only pupil variables
that related significantly with any magnitude to the CET placement
decisions were the pupils' WISC IQs."[20]

In addition to the lack of services for children exhibiting emotional or behavior problems, teachers were also concerned about
the time that assessments took. For the elementary teacher who has
a child for only one school year, the time it takes between referral

and the provision of services is particularly crucial. A number of teachers in our sample (31.8 percent) complained of the time lag between referral and evaluation. One teacher stated, "I referred one in December and another in February, and both are coming up the 10th and 11th of June." Some teachers expressed resentment at having referrals subject to various rationing devices employed by principals or other officials. For example, one teacher reported, "We were told at the beginning of the year not to recommend an evaluation unless it was absolutely urgent. They were just swamped." In another school, the teacher complained, "The teachers can recommend, but the school adjustment counselor and principal determine if a core is going to be done." Another teacher remarked, "More cores ought to be done here, but the principal is trying to keep the lid on."

Such official discouragement did not appear widespread. More general was the deterrent to referral resulting from what teachers described as the extra paperwork burden. Before a teacher referral could be acted on, a seven-page form had to be completed by the teacher, indicating the nature of the problem and the specific remedial efforts already tried in the classroom. Teachers remarked, "Our hands are tied. We see a problem in October and you don't get aid until February. We can't get any help until we get through all that paperwork." Or, "Teachers are reluctant to go along with the paperwork. For example, in order to fill out a referral, you are supposed to try four or five things in the classroom, but if it is a speech problem, I don't know how to treat that anyway. Why do I have to wait five weeks before I can complete the referral?" Another teacher remarked of her colleagues, "Teachers need to be worked with. A lot of them feel it [the referral process] is just extra work."

That teachers saw themselves as having limited discretion in referring children for evaluation was indicated in their responses to the question, "How is it decided in this school which children are to be referred for a core evaluation?" Only about a third (34.9 percent) indicated that teachers had the discretion to refer. Another 23.2 percent answered that it is up to the teacher in conjunction with the principal or one of the specialists; 23.2 percent said that it was through screening or up to the specialist, and 11.6 percent mentioned some kind of problem that would trigger a referral. Only three teachers (7 percent) said that it was up to the parent.

Despite the obstacles, teachers were responsible for a sizable percentage of all referrals for evaluation in the three systems studied. Teachers made about 42 percent of the referrals in system A and 68 percent in System C. In system B which, unlike the other two, generated a sizable proportion (about half) of its referrals through screening, teacher referrals accounted for 32 percent of the total.[21]

If the paperwork and discouragement from principals and specialists deter teachers from making referrals, what conditions motivate teachers to proceed with a referral? Teacher comments indicated that it was the disruptive child who was most likely to be referred.[22] "Those teachers who yelled the loudest when a child is a behavior problem are the ones who get cores." Or, "You don't pick up the quiet kids at the beginning of the first year." One teacher stated, "When the kids are quiet, you think they are learning." Another teacher talked of the decision to refer a child this way: "We don't refer the not-so-serious, you know, the ones who behave." Still another teacher complained, "I screamed to get LD tutoring for two kids, but it's the acting-out ones that get it first."

The analysis of student education plans supports the teachers' observations that children whose behavior presents a problem are more likely to be given priority. In both systems B and C (there was insufficient data in system A to permit a comparison), the percentage of behavior-related referrals was higher in the beginning of the school year, as was the percentage of referrals requiring a full core (more detailed) evaluation. This suggests that the more "serious" cases were referred first. In system C, behavior referrals were evaluated within a somewhat shorter time span than were other types of referral. There was, however, no significant difference in system B in the time taken to complete evaluations for behavior and learning referrals.

Another source of tension for teachers was the lack of clarity about responsibility for implementing education plans. The regulations specifically require that one person be given responsibility to see that the education plan is carried out. "For each child . . . the CET shall arrange to have one person designated as a liaison with the CET." This person is to be a member of the team who shall be responsible for "monitoring the child's progress toward reaching the goals in the educational plan and submit written reports on such progress, at least quarterly, to the child's parents, to the CET, and the principal, headmaster, director, or other head official, . . . recommend . . . any modification of such plan, . . . [and] modify the child's program in accordance with the results of any reevaluation. . . ."[23]

For each child who had been evaluated, teachers were asked, "Who is the person responsible for seeing that the various provisions of the educational plan are being carried out?" For about a third of the children (34.1 percent), the teachers either did not know or were uncertain. For another 35.6 percent of the children, one of the specialists or the principal was mentioned, and for 30.4 percent it was said to be the teacher. In other words, in more than two-thirds of the cases, either the teachers did not know who was responsible for seeing that the provisions of the education plan were carried out or they believed it was someone else's responsibility.

While some teachers and many specialists reported excellent working relations, a lack of coordination between teacher and specialist was cited as a problem by a number of teachers. For example, "I get no feedback from the resource room," or, "No one has ever followed up with me about Pamela," or "I don't get any feedback from the school adjustment counselor. It may be a time problem, but maybe it is just him."

When a child is assigned to several different specialists, the problem of fragmentation may have consequences for the teacher as well as for the child. For example, several teachers expressed concern about coordination with several specialists working with an individual child. As one put it, "There are too many specialists; it puts a stigma on kids singled out." Another teacher suggested, "We need more time to get together with specialists for overall considerations. It might be better to have one specialist for many needs."

Teacher-Specialist Relations

An implicit assumption in the utilization of multidisciplinary teams for the evaluation of children is that all members contribute equally according to their special knowledge and experience with the child. This assumption ignores the status and other differences among team members. Such differences underlie the tensions between teachers and specialists reported by teachers and observed in the CET meetings.

The specialist can provide some relief for the teacher in handling a classroom problem. However, there are costs to the teacher in seeking such help. Teachers resent the time it takes to get services of specialists through the core evaluation process and the added paperwork of a teacher-initiated referral. That teachers are concerned about relations with specialists is evident in the response to the question about needed improvements in the core evaluation process: nearly half (19, or 43 percent) voiced concern about the specialist's role.[24] Tensions between regular and special education personnel reached the point in some instances where they would refuse even to communicate with one another. The Massachusetts Legislature's Special Commission on Chapter 766 reported as follows:

There is some evidence of separate factions within a school system between regular and special education teachers (e.g., the feeling of a regular education teacher that a special education teacher is "out to get my job," or special education teachers who feel that regular education teachers dump unnecessary problems on them). In some cases, there are separate lunch hours for regular . . . and special education teachers.[25]

A number of factors inherent in the situations of specialists and teachers contribute to the tension between them.

Teacher Isolation
A particularly salient element in the teacher's situation is that he or she works during most of the day in isolation from other adults. Whatever interaction takes place with peers is generally limited to informal socializing that may occur at lunchtime or during an occasional coffee break in the teachers' lounge. Teaching is a lonely occupation as well as a demanding one. The teacher constantly has to deal with his or her charges with few breaks during the day for relaxation or reflection. Given this isolation, the core evaluation process, at least in theory, seems to offer an opportunity for the

teacher to obtain information, advice, and perhaps help from specialists, as well as parents, in dealing with individual children. However, a number of additional factors deter the teacher from making use of this potential resource.

An Indeterminant Technology and Product

Another unique feature of the teacher's situation is that the object of his or her work is the child. Whatever skills and effort the teacher brings to the classroom are aimed at enhancing the knowledge of the child or modifying the child's behavior. Change within the child is the product of the teacher's work.

The core evaluation process may offer somewhat mixed benefits for the teacher. On the one hand, it may provide a chance to get some additional help for a child. On the other hand, particularly if the teacher is initiating the referral, it may represent an admission that the teacher is unable to correct the problem. In a sense it is an admission of failure. Should the referral be initiated elsewhere, by the parent or by a specialist, it may be perceived by the teacher as an accusation. The child has problems that the teacher has failed to correct or adequately handle; furthermore the teacher has not considered the problems sufficiently serious to warrant a referral or he or she would have done so already.

I observed teachers on several occasions entering core evaluation meetings making excuses about their failure to identify problems in instances where referrals had been generated elsewhere. Some teachers were also defensive about having initiated referrals. This defensiveness was reflected in the child-blame engaged in by many of the teachers observed in team meetings.

That the product of the teacher's work is change within the child has another consequence for the core evaluation process. Teachers may be reluctant to pass on an inferior product against which they may be judged by their peers. Passing children to the next grade without having adequately prepared them could reflect on the ability of the teacher. Part of the responsibility may be deflected to the child or on the family or home situation. In such instances the child's school records may be developed and used to support the assessment of blame. As one teacher put it, "When I see a fat folder on a child, I know I've got problems coming." The thick record is itself a visible sign that the child may be expected to present problems beyond the normal abilities of the classroom teacher to solve. The record, ostensibly a tool to aid those working with the child, may serve to condition the official view of the child as a "problem" and therefore perhaps beyond help.

Time Perspectives
Teachers and specialists have differing time perspectives with regard to the ordering and completion of their work responsibilities. Teachers, at least in the lower grades, have only a ten-month period to work with a child before passing him or her to the next teacher. Other school personnel can afford the luxury of a longer view. The specialists and principal can generally expect to have a child under their jurisdiction over a period of years. Thus whatever happens during any one year may not be seen by the specialist or principal as particularly crucial. After all, if a problem is not corrected this year, one can continue to work on it the following year or the year after. Some problems may simply disappear as a result of maturation. The teacher, however, has to do whatever he or she is going to do with the child within ten months.

The regular class teacher, while having less time than others to effect change, also has more time. The teacher may have responsibility for a child for only a fraction of the child's total school career, but the teacher, unlike other school personnel, is responsible for the child for most of each school day throughout the ten-month school year. That the teacher has a child for large blocks of time during the day may amplify the impact of disruptive behavior. Sending the child to specialists may provide temporary relief for at least part of the day and week. However, it may also permit the teacher to abdicate responsibility for the child's problem. After all, the team decision, typically made with only token participation of the classroom teacher, has been to address the presenting problems by referring the child to one or more specialists. Individualized education programs in Massachusetts and elsewhere are rarely concerned with the regular education portion of the child's program.[26] The implication is that the specialist has some expertise that the classroom teacher does not have. While the specialist's consultative role to the teacher may be discussed, the specialist rarely acts as a consultant because of the strong structural and role constraints that keep them apart. Among these constraints are differences in their respective rank and status.

Status Differences

Specialists often have qualifications as classroom teachers, but they also have additional education and certification. These additional credentials frequently bring the specialists higher pay than teachers. (In fact, in many states, special class teachers with the same training and experience as regular class teachers generally receive higher pay.) In addition, the specialists and teachers are responsible to different administrative hierarchies. The classroom teacher, particularly at the elementary level, is responsible to the principal. The principal evaluates the teacher and makes recommendations for tenure or promotion. The considerable power of the principal over teachers was suggested by one teacher who pointed out, "He assigns extra work to nontenured teachers. For example, audiovisual, traffic, supplies, and so forth. Technically, under the contract, you don't have to do it. But if you want tenure, you do."

The specialist is subject to the authority of the principal only insofar as he or she is working in the building for which the principal is responsible. The specialist must defer to the principal in matters of space, scheduling, and access to personnel. However, the specialists are administratively responsible to a program director or division head close to the top of the system's central administrative hierarchy. Furthermore specialists usually serve more than one school, so that whatever difficulties they may encounter in one work situation may be compensated for by experiences in other schools.

The status differential between teacher and specialist is reflected in teachers' reports of intimidation in encounters with specialists during the education plan meetings. The teacher is at a disadvantage in the assessment process because of his or her relative unfamiliarity with the law and procedures, and the specialists' use of unfamiliar terminology.[27] The teacher, like the parents, is outnumbered and is an outsider temporarily joining an ongoing group that has established some effective solidarity and group norms unknown to the teacher.

Lack of Services

An additional source of tension is undoubtedly that teachers looking for help with children who disturb the classroom or otherwise require special attention are not getting it. This lack of service was demonstrated in the differences between teachers' descriptions of problems and services received by children. While a large number of the children were seen by teachers as having emotional or behavior problems, most services were directed toward learning problems.

Authority over Children

Perhaps the most salient issue contributing to tensions between specialists and teachers is that of authority over the child. Teachers are subject to conflicting pressures. On the one hand, teachers may wish to relinquish responsibility for children who are disruptive. On the other hand, the teacher may view himself or herself as the primary person responsible for the child and may resent intrusion from outsiders. One teacher put it this way:

The first- and second-grade teachers here had a list of five or six kids who ought to be retained [not promoted]. However, the psychologist recommended promotion on the basis of IQ tests. Teachers are losing their identity. We used to have teacher aides here who were paid $100 a week and that worked fine. Now they have to hire special tutors at $6.75 per hour.

Interviews with specialists revealed a number of instances of close working relations between individual teachers and specialists, but a more typical pattern is that the child is sent from the classroom to a specialist who works with the child on a particular problem. Responsibility for the problem is in a sense transferred from teacher to specialist.

Conclusion

These findings suggest a paradoxical limitation in the assessment process and in the development and implementation of the education program. Except for children placed in special classes or private schools, the regular class teacher is the central dispenser of education and should presumably therefore play a key role in identifying, referring, planning for, and serving children with special needs. This central role is particularly important for a special education policy that seeks to bring children with special needs into the regular education mainstream. Instead the teacher's role is marginal compared with that of the specialist who dominates the processing of children. The result is an abdication of responsibility for dealing with the child's problem in the regular classroom and a fragmentation of services to the individual child. One observer has stated the problem as follows:

The referral of a child to a specialist outside the individual building does not in any sense represent the identification of the child as handicapped; rather, it represents a calculated decision that, even with good effort, the building personnel do not expect to be able to serve a particular child well at the time he or she needs help. The personnel making the referral have measured themselves as well as the child.[28]

Thus several factors inherent in teachers' and specialists' respective situations limit the teachers' role. Teachers operate in relative isolation, using an indeterminate technology to accomplish educational objectives within a short time frame. They are concerned about being evaluated by peers, parents, specialists, and administrators on the results of their efforts and are protective of their authority over the children in their charge. They may be only too willing, however, to relinquish responsibility to specialists for treating problems that appear to require expertise or resources beyond those the teacher can provide. The specialist, on the other hand, enjoys a higher status and operates under less severe time constraints and with what appears to be a more scientific and precise technology.

Attempts to limit the number of handicapped children permitted in a regular class may be important in some school systems to prevent a precipitous shifting of children from self-contained special classes.[29] However, such measures fail to address the problem of redefining the teachers' role as more central in treating the whole child.

7
Reform Objectives versus Bureaucratic Realities

I have focused to this point on the referral and assessment process and development of the educational plan. The analysis has suggested that the principal actors, constrained by the need to adapt to an overwhelming work load, employed job-coping mechanisms that tended to distort the policy outcomes provided in the law and regulations. Yet it would be naive to suppose that any law can achieve 100 percent compliance, particularly a law that seeks to change the behavior of thousands of personnel operating in a highly decentralized bureaucratic structure. It is possible that these street-level bureaucrats, while devising individual solutions to increased work loads that deviated in some procedural respects from the letter of the law and regulations, nonetheless dispensed services closely approximating the law's intent. In this chapter I shall compare the law's broad reform provisions with the experience of the three school systems in implementing them. Specifically I shall consider the objectives of Chapter 766 with respect to mainstreaming, more efficient identification, more uniform and comprehensive processing of children with special needs, the provision of increased and individually planned services, and the elimination of labeling. As with the rest of the analysis, I shall consider how the need to process people on a mass basis affects the implementation of these objectives.

Mainstreaming

Martin J. Kaufman et al. summarized the case for mainstreaming; it is based on the belief that it will remove stigma from handicapped youngsters, enhance their social status, facilitate modeling of appropriate behavior, provide a more stimulating and competitive environment, offer a more flexible, cost-effective service in the child's own neighborhood, and be more acceptable to the public, particularly minority groups.[1]

Chapter 766 required that children with special needs be placed in regular education programs to the maximum extent feasible, if even for just a fraction of the school day. Special classes, where necessary, were to be located within regular school facilities.[2] Under PL 94-142, state education agencies must now ensure

1. that to the maximum extent appropriate, handicapped children, including children in public or private institutions or other care facilities, are educated with children who are not handicapped, and
2. that special classes, separate schooling, or other removal of handicapped children from the regular education environment occurs only when the nature or severity of the handicap is such that education in regular classes with the use of supplementary aids and services cannot be achieved satisfactorily.[3]

These provisions, designed to end the segregation of handicapped children, have evoked fears on the part of regular class teachers that special classes would be closed, thus returning numbers of difficult children to regular classrooms.

The specter of hordes of handicapped children being loosed upon regular class teachers never materialized in Massachusetts. First, there were probably not that many children in full-time, self-contained separate programs. For the year ending June 1974 the three systems studied reported a combined total of 128 children in "substantially separate" programs, that is, programs with integration into regular education programs less than 25 percent of the time. This number is from a total combined enrollment of 26,683 (for the 1973–74 school year), thus amounting to about 0.5 percent.[4]

Furthermore the regulations contained a grandfather clause whereby all children in special programs as of September 1974 were presumed to be correctly placed unless and until evidence was presented to the contrary.[5] This provision was developed at least partly in response to fears of some parents that their children might have services taken from them under the new law.[6]

Statewide, the first year of implementation of Chapter 766 actually resulted in a shifting of children from less to *more* restrictive program prototypes as indicated by data obtained from a state Department of Education official. This shift probably reflects in part the increased use of resource rooms. Table 8 shows the percentage of children with special needs reported by local systems throughout the state in various program prototypes as of October 1974 and October 1975.

The Massachusetts special education funding mechanism operates in a way that actually makes it more advantageous for local education agencies with high special education costs to place chil-

Table 8
Special Needs Children by Program Prototype

	October 1974	October 1975
In Regular Class with Support, No Time Out (%)	35.9	19.8
In Regular Class with up to 25 Percent Time Out (%)	43.9	56.2
In Regular Class less than 75 Percent of the Time (%)	20.2	24.0
Total	100.0	100.0

Source: Data supplied to the author by an official of the Massachusetts State Department of Education.

dren in more restrictive settings that bring higher reimbursements.[7] This outcome is similar to the initial experience of Florida under its pupil-weighting system adopted in 1973. The Florida system provides greater state aid for children in more restrictive settings; as a result,

There has been "a definite tendency to assign exceptional students to full-time self-contained classrooms instead of attempting to integrate them into part-time basic classroom situations.". . . In a survey of local school district personnel, the Florida Department of Education found that 12 percent of all principals interviewed "reported that they had received direct pressure from 'above' to retain children in full-time classes rather than place them in resource room situations."[8]

But the problem does not end here. There is also evidence from Massachusetts that in order to staff additional resource rooms at minimal cost, administrators were reassigning untrained regular education teachers to operate them. It is no wonder that some resource rooms are used as "dumping grounds" and "detention centers" instead of offering the individual instruction for which they are intended.[9]

The major impact of both the Massachusetts and federal laws on mainstreaming is probably the establishment of procedural barriers to the inappropriate assignment of children to self-contained classes or, to put it less charitably, the arbitrary sorting and dumping of children troublesome to regular class teachers. During the study several instances of active recruitment of children by special class teachers were noted. On one occasion teachers of a separate program strongly intervened in a core evaluation, saying that they would like the girl being assessed assigned to their program as they needed more girls to provide a balanced sex ratio. In another instance a newly assigned resource room teacher participated in all core evaluations in her school until she got enough children for her program. One special class teacher was instructed by a core evaluation team chairperson to write an education plan for a child whom she had not yet seen. The child was transferring from outside the system and, although he had not yet been evaluated, special class placement was deemed appropriate on the basis of an interview with the parents and an informal verbal opinion from the previous school, where he had been enrolled in a regular class. The special class teacher, when he asked what he should say in the plan, was told simply, "You know what to say. Just say the same thing you would for any other child like this." In each of these situations the staff was engaged in creative problem solving that seemed perfectly logical from their perspectives.

Such instances were rare, not only because of a lack of space in existing special classes, but more importantly because of the genuine professional commitment of most special education administrators and special class teachers to mainstreaming and the least restrictive environment concept. Such a commitment had existed even before the passage of the law; however, Chapter 766 provided special educators the necessary leverage with principals and regular education administrators to expand and revamp services and get the special classes "out of the basements." Such efforts have not been universally successful, as indicated by the findings of a special legislative commission studying Chapter 766:

Although regulations specifically describe location, type, and size of room where special education services should be rendered, some LEAs [local education agencies] persist in servicing the special needs population in closet-like rooms which are isolated in the basement.[10]

There was evidence of a more subtle kind of dumping taking place under the new law. There appeared to be a wholesale shifting of responsibility for troublesome children from the regular class teacher to a specialist or resource room teacher.

I observed numerous instances of close working relations between regular class teachers and specialists. Specialists would consult teachers on how to handle classroom problems and how best to work with individual children. Some effort would be made to coordinate learning in the regular class with the specialist's intervention with a particular child. However, the maintenance of such relationships required additional time, which was in short supply.

Far more frequently the teacher had little contact with specialists, no knowledge of the content of the education plan, and an attitude that the child's learning or behavior problem was the responsibility of someone else, namely the specialist. Even when specialists sought to work closely with teachers, the pressures of increasing case loads and vastly increased time spent in the assessment process prevented them from doing so. Thus the law that sought to limit the segregation of handicapped children contributed to their further isolation and increased the danger that such children might be stigmatized on the basis of their need for help from a specialist outside the regular classroom.

More Efficient Identification and Processing of Children with Special Needs

According to state Department of Education estimates, only 50 to 60 percent of children with special needs had been identified and provided services by Massachusetts schools before Chapter 766.[11] The regulations require local education authorities to undertake a number of activities to identify children in need of special services.[12] These include public information campaigns, development and implementation of a case-finding plan, annual screening of kindergarten and prekindergarten children, orientation workshops for parents, continual in-school screening of school-age children, and the maintenance of a register and census of children with special needs. Although there was no shortage of referrals from teachers and parents, the systems studied took seriously their responsibilities for identifying children with special needs, particularly provisions pertaining to screening kindergarten and prekindergarten children. Local special education officials shared a concern for early identification and treatment of problems that might hinder learning. Nonetheless there was considerable variation in how this concern was carried out. While system B derived more than half its referrals from pre- and in-school screening, screening in the other two systems accounted for but a fraction of referrals. Furthermore the kinds of disorder identified through screening were directly related to the specialty of the person doing the screening. For example, system B, which relied much more heavily on speech specialists to conduct screening than the other two systems, referred more than twice as many children for evaluations for speech problems. Thus the availability and deployment of certain specially trained staff accounted for variations in the frequencies and types of disorder picked up and referred for evaluation.

Those doing the screening in many instances were actually referring children to themselves. That is, the same speech or learning disabilities specialist conducting screening would participate in the evaluation and eventually treat the child picked up in screening. Thus there can be an element of circularity about the identification-assessment-treatment process, particularly when implanted in a categorical system. Children referred for "learning disabilities" problems are likely to be given learning disabilities tests and found to need learning disabilities services.[13] School systems need to guard not only against failing to identify children in need of services, but also against including in the special education network children who do not need special services.

One measure of the relative efficiency of the assessment process is the time required to complete an assessment of an individual child. The Massachusetts regulations require that the evaluation take place within thirty working days after the parents are informed or no more than thirty-five days after the child is referred for evaluation. The parents are to receive a written notice of the results within ten days of completion of the evaluation and may have an additional forty-five days to decide whether to accept or reject the plan.[14] Thus a total of ninety working days is provided between referral and written acceptance or rejection of the educational plan by the parents.[15]

Despite substantial differences among the three systems with regard to case-finding and assessment procedures and staff available for assessment, there was a surprising uniformity in the time taken to complete the assessments. The mean number of months taken to complete the assessments was 6.9 in system A, 7.8 in system B, and 7.9 in system C—all considerably longer than the thirty-five days (or three months if one considers the time until the plan must be signed by the parent) permitted under the law.[16]

For systems B and C where data were available, only 11.9 and 21.2 percent of referrals, respectively, were completed within three months. These figures should be taken not as a criticism of the schools but as an index of the overwhelming scope of the task confronting them. System B, which had the most effective record-keeping procedures, had completed evaluations on 539 children. However, it also had a nearly equal number of cases for whom the assessment procedure had *not* been completed as of early July 1975.[17] This number included some that were simply awaiting a parent's signature on the educational plan; most, however, were still awaiting core evaluation team assessment. Nearly half of these had been referred within three months of the end of the school year; but the majority had been referred earlier, some as early as the previous September. The special education administrator was well aware of the problem and planned to assign extra staff during the summer months to eliminate the backlog by the opening of school in the fall.

Equity, Uniformity, and Comprehensive Coverage

As stated in the Massachusetts legislation,

It is the purpose of this act to provide for a flexible and uniform system of special education program opportunities for all children requiring special education; to provide a flexible and non-discrim-inatory system for identifying and evaluating the individual needs of children requiring special education; . . . and to prevent denials of equal educational opportunity on the basis of national origin, sex, economic status, race, religion, and physical or mental handicap and the provision of differential education services.[18]

Chapter 766 thereby seeks to end arbitrary and discriminatory classification and assignment through an individualized approach to children with special needs. However, this approach is to be accomplished in a way that assures a measure of equity, that is, equal treatment for children with the same needs and responsiveness to parents and teachers who are involved in planning for individual children. Fiscal constraints and the governance of local school systems impose on the schools the additional requirements of accountability and fiscal integrity. These aims—equity, responsiveness, accountability, efficiency, and fiscal integrity—constitute conflicting bureaucratic requirements.[19] As might be expected, the three school systems studied pursued strategies that maximized one or another of these requirements at some sacrifice to the others.

In the absence of any specific guidance from the state Department of Education, any number of core evaluation team (CET) models would have been consistent with the regulations. Not surprisingly, there were considerable differences between school systems in the handling of the core evaluation process.

One serious problem with the implementation of the mandate for uniform treatment was the absence of any explicit system of priority in the referral, assessment, and provision of services for children with special needs. Except for the distinctions between full and intermediate core evaluations, the regulations, directives of the state Department of Education, and the explicit policies of the school systems studied provided no differentiation between more or less urgent cases. It was as if all children were to be processed at once, without official regard to the relative seriousness of each situation. The child with multiple physical and emotional problems was to be processed no sooner than the child with a slight hearing impairment.

The federal law, PL 94–142, requires that local education agencies first use federal funds available under the act to serve previously unserved children. Only after all such children have been served may the funds be used to augment programs for other handicapped children, starting with those having the most severe handicap in each disability category.[20] While this provision still allows considerable local discretion in determining specific priorities, it at least addresses the problem of setting priorities on services in a way the Massachusetts law failed to do.

All three school systems made unofficial distinctions between routine and more complex cases. Routine cases were viewed by school personnel—teachers and specialists—as those in which the completion of the educational plan form was necessary in order to provide the services of a specialist. In these cases an implicit decision that a service was needed would be made before referral. The evaluation was then viewed as a bureaucratic hurdle to be gotten over as quickly as possible, in some cases even without the supposedly mandatory participation of parents. Many of these meetings took on a contrived, routine character. As a psychologist described the procedure followed in one elementary school, "We [the specialists] normally decide what to do with kids without all of the legalistic terms and paperwork, and we get things done quicker. If a kid needs services requiring a core [evaluation], we just call one the next day and get together to fill out the forms." Not surprisingly, this school was among those in the system with the fewest number of evaluations.

In the face of an overwhelming increase in the work load brought on by Chapter 766, many rationing techniques were unofficially employed to hold down the number of referrals. These included the following.

1. A failure of teachers to refer, despite evidence of problems that should have indicated the need for an evaluation of a child. Teachers were deterred by the necessity to complete the forms and to justify their assessment of the problem to the principal and specialists. An acknowledgment of a problem they could not handle themselves represented to some teachers an acknowledgment of failure. Teachers could look forward to the end of the school year when they would pass the children to the next teacher; consequently many tended to refer only the most troublesome.

2. Parents would occasionally be dissuaded by the principal from requesting a core evaluation, with assurances that the child was "doing fine" or that services were already being provided.

3. Teacher-initiated referrals would simply not be processed by principals or specialists. Referrals from teachers were generally submitted through the principal or specialists, and in a number of

instances the principal or specialist would simply fail to follow through.

4. Administrators would informally instruct subordinates to cut back on referrals. For example, in one school system, principals having the largest number of referrals were told by the administration to curtail evaluations because of concerns about the costs of services recommended by the evaluation teams.

There is no way to determine exactly how widespread such practices have been. There was considerable variation among the three systems and among schools within the systems. However, all three systems were certainly taxed beyond previous requirements; the rationing was justified by the felt necessity to avoid a breakdown of the processing system and to insure the physical and mental well-being of the staff.[21]

In general, these rationing techniques took the form of unsanctioned informal categorization of potential referrals in terms of the utility of the referral for the personnel most directly involved. For each individual making such a decision, a weighing of the relative costs and benefits of an evaluation might take into account criteria such as the following.

I. Concern for the well-being of the child. This concern needs to be emphasized lest it be concluded that school personnel operated only out of self-interest. Concern for children was without question the foremost consideration for the great majority of school personnel. Without such concern implementation would have broken down completely, for administrators and specialists in all three school systems kept the process going by working extraordinarily long hours under constant stress with little hope of catching up, at least during the first year or two.

2. The institutional rewards for referrals. Some principals reported their belief that they would be evaluated at least informally on the number of referrals processed by their schools. Principals in systems B and C were encouraged to refer; those in system A were not.

3. The degree to which children were creating problems for teachers or other personnel because of disruptive behavior. Teachers generally stated that they referred the "loudest" children first. This report was confirmed by an examination of the dates of referral of

learning and behavior problems. In systems B and C, where sufficient data were available, behavior referrals occurred with relatively
greater frequency in the first three months of the school year. Also,
in system C, which took a more individualized approach to the evaluation process, behavior problems were evaluated more rapidly.
Sixteen percent of children referred for learning problems in system C were evaluated in less than four months, while thirty-two
percent of those with behavior problems were evaluated in less
than four months. (In system B, which had a more routinized and
less individualized referral and assessment process, there were no
major differences in the time required to process learning and behavior problems.)

4. The position of the person interested in the evaluation. The
speed of processing tended to be affected by the position of the
person making the referral. Parent and principal referrals, while
accounting for a relatively small percentage of the total, were generally processed more rapidly than teacher referrals.[22]

School personnel faced requirements to process many more
children than they possibly could but were not given priorities by
state or local authorities. Under the circumstances these parochial
considerations, serving the psychological and work-related needs of
school personnel, operated to establish priorities that the law and
state administrators had failed to set.

Systems varied in their rate of referral and processing, as did
individual schools within the same system. By the end of June 1975
system A had completed evaluations on about 3.8 percent of its students, system B, 5.5 percent, and system C, 2.8 percent. (Statewide,
systems evaluated from as few as 1 percent to 25 percent of their
students.[23]) Some individual schools referred and evaluated no children, while others processed many. The mean age of children evaluated varied from 12.6 years in system A to 7.5 years in system B and
10.3 years in system C. Of schools in systems B and C that had
evaluated at least five children, some completed nearly half within
the required three-month period, others completed none. Speech
problems were the primary reason for referral for about 20 percent
of children evaluated in system B but only 5 percent in system A and
less than 2 percent in system C. While learning referrals were rela-

tively constant across the three systems, ranging from 58.1 to 65.9 percent of referrals, behavior referrals accounted for 22.2 percent in system A, 13.6 percent in system B, and 29.2 percent in system C.

A law and regulations intended to produce a uniform application of procedures instead in certain respects yielded wide variations in application. The chances of a child's being referred, evaluated, and provided special education services were associated with such presumably extraneous factors as the relative wealth of the community in which he or she lived, the child's disruptiveness or submissiveness in class, his or her age, sex,[24] the sex of the teacher,[25] the aggressiveness and socioeconomic status of the parents, the current availability and cost of services needed, and the presence in the school system of particular categories of specialists.

Such variations in the identification and treatment of children with special needs are by no means unique to Massachusetts. During the 1976–77 school year children served under PL 94–142 ranged from a low of 4.55 percent of school-age children in Mississippi to 11.48 percent in Utah.[26] Such statewide averages, reported for purposes of reimbursement under PL 94–142, mask wide-ranging local variations in the number of children identified and served and in the nature and quality of services. Wilken and Callahan have described the situation this way:

Disparities in special education services can be found in states of every condition. Disparities are common to states that are rich, that are poor, that are urban, that are rural. Disparities persist whether states spend a great deal for special education or very little. Disparities persist whether states educate most handicapped children or relatively few. Indeed, there is some evidence that service disparities may be growing wider with every additional dollar spent and every additional handicapped child served.[27]

Parent Involvement and Interdisciplinary Team Assessment

The Massachusetts and federal laws seek to regulate arbitrary and inappropriate classification and assignment of children by restricting the use of standardized tests and by requiring joint assessment and planning by a team including parents, teachers, administrators, and specialists such as medical doctors or nurses, psychologists, social workers or school adjustment counselors, learning disabilities, speech, hearing, mobility, or other specialists as needed. Ideally all contribute information about the child's strengths, resources, potential, and specific deficits from the differing perspectives of their professional backgrounds and unique experiences with the child. The net effect of these required procedures in the three school systems studied has been a greater involvement of parents, a more careful assessment of children, and some genuine team decision making. At the same time both teachers and parents play a secondary role in relation to specialists in the evaluation process.[28]

The increased parent involvement was acknowledged even by school personnel who felt the procedural requirements an unnecessary burden, as their schools were "already involving parents." The impact of parent participation was both real and anticipatory. In numerous instances parents made a substantial contribution to the assessment and planning process but frequently anticipatory actions were taken by school personnel to placate or avoid conflict with parents.

The relative efficacy of parent involvement is directly related to their socioeconomic status. The more affluent and professional the parents, the more likely school personnel are to pay attention to them and adhere to procedural requirements. Such parents are also more likely than poor parents to possess the resources—self-assurance, time, money, knowledge, and advocacy-group support—necessary to influence school decisions. They also have the advantage of living in communities that have more highly developed services. This is not to say that the children of affluent parents are invariably served well and those of the poor are served poorly. I observed too many exceptions to such a generalization. However, the implementation of special education reform is strongly biased in favor of children of middle- and upper-income parents.

This analysis of education program meetings, supported by subsequent studies of the process in Massachusetts and other states, suggests that the interdisciplinary team assessments do not usually work as intended. Decisions are sometimes made before team meetings, undue weight is given to standardized test scores, one or two individuals dominate the deliberations, parents and teachers have only token involvement, and service priorities are dictated by cost, local tradition, and the relative strength and status of various categories of educational professionals.

However, IEP meetings serve functions other than assessment and prescription for individual children. These meetings may also be status-conferring ceremonies and political bargaining sessions. From these additional perspectives, much of what I observed makes sense. Team deliberations often appeared ritualistic; participants, except parents and most teachers, often seemed to be playing out roles they had rehearsed earlier or played in previous assessment meetings. School personnel frequently acted as if the meetings, the paperwork, the involvement of parents, and other procedural requirements were so many obstacles to be gotten over as quickly as possible. In fact, the IEPs do serve a ceremonial function. They provide official sanction for public school to treat certain children differently. Since the consequences for the child and parents may be severe, it is important that the appearance of procedural fairness and diagnostic rigor be preserved, even when they are substantively absent from the proceedings. The ceremony serves to reassure all participants that the child is indeed protected from arbitrary treatment by the processing organization. Such reassurance is important to the participating education professionals, as well as to parents and the community at large. Educators, to assuage the multiple stresses inherent in performance of their professional roles, need to feel that what they are doing is indeed proper and in the best interests of the child.

From a political perspective, the IEP team meetings may be seen as the locus of a bureaucratic struggle over power and status, control of time, money, staff, and other resources. The IEP process described in state and federal law evokes the image of equals whose joint deliberations are directed only at securing the best possible service for the child. The reality suggests that each member brings to the team meeting a personal agenda, generally hidden, that may conflict with that of the other participants and may have little to do with the child. The principal may seek to maximize or minimize placements or limit services in keeping with administrative considerations directed toward limiting costs and maximizing state and federal reimbursements. Teachers may hope to find relief from having to contend with a troublesome child; specialists may wish to recruit children to demonstrate the importance of their particular specialty; parents may hope to extract services beyond those the school is willing to offer; all categories of school personnel may seek to guard their respective work environments from the intrusion of administrators, colleagues, or parents. Many of the techniques conventionally thought to belong in the legislative cloakrooms may be observed here: coalition building, caucusing, lobbying outside the formal meetings, the selective use of information including technical expertise, trading "pork-barrel" rewards, and mobilization of outside support groups. Not all participants are equally adept at employing these tactics, nor do all start with equal resources. Most important, the child generally is not there. The nature of the representation of the child calls into question the sufficiency of the planning and assessment process and attendant procedural safeguards to advance and protect the interests of the child.

Increased and Individualized Services

Much of the controversy and effort in the first year's operation under Chapter 766 concerned the assessment process, yet the ultimate purpose was the provision of services to provide maximum support for each handicapped child to learn in the most appropriate and least restrictive setting. School systems were required to provide whatever services were recommended by the core evaluation team without being constrained by cost considerations.[29] If appropriate services were unavailable, the school system would have to develop them, purchase them, or send the child outside the system at local expense to wherever such services could be obtained. This remarkable provision might be expected to break down in practice by the informal imposition of cost calculations or a restriction on the number of children to whom it would apply, but one may still legitimately inquire about the extent to which the spirit of the provision was honored by observing the salience of cost considerations in core evaluation deliberations.

These requirements immediately expanded the range of options and did lead to some expansion and redesign of special education services. Several examples of innovative and imaginative use of support services for youngsters with special needs were witnessed: a preschool program operated jointly by two school systems, a high school vocational program, a new special class for previously institutionalized developmentally disabled children, the hiring of a mobility specialist to assist children with gross motor problems, the purchase of outside medical and psychological services for some students, and the referral of children at school expense to a commercially operated physical culture and self-defense program. All three school systems were taking steps to decentralize special classes into neighborhood schools. Systems B and C also established several additional resource rooms; and all three systems hired additional tutors, generally on an hourly basis.

A measure of the success of core evaluation teams in providing new services was the wish of school superintendents and the Department of Education to stop what Associate Commissioner Audette termed "runaway CETs."[30] He was referring to the legal obligation of the special education administrator to provide whatever services the evaluation team recommended regardless of the cost or current availability within the school system. In June 1975 the Department of Education proposed changes in the regulations which, among other things, would have given special education administrators veto power over CET recommendations.[31]

In some respects the implementation of Chapter 766 actually resulted in a diminution of services. One problem was the wholesale withdrawal of services to school children by other state agencies. Special education administrators throughout the state complained bitterly of instances in which services previously offered to children at little or no cost were now being withdrawn or offered on a fee basis. Agencies cited included the departments of welfare, public health, mental health, and the Massachusetts Rehabilitation Commission. According to testimony of special education administrators, agencies that previously provided direct services to handicapped children "now withdraw these services from school-aged students and act simply as a referral agency to the public school."[32] While other agencies were more circumspect, the commissioner of the Massachusetts Rehabilitation Commission put it in writing to his staff:

Massachusetts Rehabilitation Commission reconfirms its policy not to provide paid services to clients who are covered by the provisions of Chapter 766, that is, students with special needs who are under age 22 and not graduated from high school.[33]

The problem, as described by the legislature's special commission on Chapter 766, was that responsibility for certain school-age clients served by these other agencies had been transferred to the schools. However, there was no concurrent transfer of funds or increased appropriations to local education agencies to provide the additional services.[34] As a result, relations between schools and other human services agencies at the state and local levels have been characterized by sometimes rancorous debate over programmatic and fiscal responsibility for individual and categorically defined groups of children. As one observer noted, "More children were in the cracks than in the programs."[35]

Despite much attention to the problem of interagency coordination, there has been little improvement. State human service agencies take the position that in the absence of funding from the legislature, they do not have to carry out certain legislatively mandated services. The Massachusetts Department of Education in response has taken the unusual step of filing a suit protesting the state's failure to appropriate funds to implement human service laws.[36]

The Office for Children, the state agency established to monitor and coordinate services for children, has been less than effective. It has been plagued by problems of increasing bureaucratization, lack of direct authority over other agencies, and a focus on individual cases to the relative neglect of broad programmatic issues.[37] The experience of the Massachusetts Office for Children has prompted one investigator to suggest that "watchdog agencies are allowed to bark but not bite."[38]

One can appreciate the sense of futility that must at times affect even the most optimistic public servant confronting the abundance of organizations and programs that together offer such a dearth of services for children with special needs. The frustration of those trying to ameliorate the situation through better coordination or schemes for improved dissemination of program information is symbolized by the following incident. Department of Education staff labored long and hard to compile a directory of human service programs for children with special needs available through state and local agencies. The directory was intended for distribution to local education agencies. When completed, the budget item for printing had been depleted. By the time printing funds were again found, the directory was thought to be too dated to be useful, and the staff had to begin immediately the process of revising it.[39]

The dismal experience of Massachusetts with coordination of human services for children is likely to be repeated in other states. Under PL 94–142, state education agencies are responsible for coordinating all education and support services for handicapped children "in order to assure a simple line of responsibility with regard to the education of handicapped children."[40] The magnitude of such a responsibility is suggested by the following:

One contributor to the complexity of special education program operation is the presence of a highly fractionated set of federal programs for handicapped children. As the U.S. General Accounting Office pointed out in a recent study, federal programs for handi- capped children are so numerous and operated through so many different agencies that most programs operate as if the others didn't exist.[41]

Federal law requires coordination at the state level; however, there is no comparable requirement for coordination of federal programs for handicapped children.[42]

The withdrawal of ancillary services by the state agencies created serious problems for the schools; perhaps even more demoralizing for school personnel was the reduction of in-school services re- sulting from the reallocation of staff resources to complete core evaluations. The specialists who conducted assessments and partic- ipated in education plan meetings were also responsible for pro- viding services recommended by the evaluation teams. These spe- cialists, along with other team members, faced two problems. One was the sheer volume of new assessments; the second was the vastly increased time required to test or otherwise evaluate each child, write up the assessment report, attend the team meetings, and write the education plan. Rationing devices were sometimes employed to avoid this time-consuming process altogether. More frequently, assessments would be routinized. For example, the language em- ployed to report test results was standardized; similar cases would be described in almost identical terms. Meetings were conducted in a cursory fashion. Parent signatures were obtained on blank forms to eliminate the extra time required to get the signed education plans returned. Education plans, instead of offering individualized programs, most often did little more than list various specialists the child would visit throughout the week.

The most frequent response to the overwhelming work load was to work harder and longer hours at school and complete the paperwork at home. Specialists were caught in a particularly difficult bind. Their contribution was essential to the assessment process. At the same time, a conscientious discharge of the assessment and planning responsibilities meant less time to work with children and more time completing forms. As one specialist said, "It just kills me to walk by those kids with them saying, 'Aren't you coming to see us today?' "

The considerable personal strain on front-line staff was quite apparent. Additional staff were hired in all three systems, but the added staff was rarely sufficient to meet the increased demand. That the Massachusetts law was implemented as well as it was is due to the dedication of those at the local level whose extra effort constituted a sizable hidden subsidy to the state.

Just as there was informal rationing of referrals in order to control the work flow, there was also rationing of specialist services following assessments.

1. Services previously offered on an individual basis were now delivered in groups. Specialists often rationalized such modifications as better for the children. A learning disabilities specialist explained, for example, "Sandra can benefit from participating in a tutoring group since she needs to work on interpersonal problems." It is hardly accidental that this theoretical breakthrough in treatment modality was coincident with the additional burdens placed on special education personnel by Chapter 766.

2. The number of sessions per week and time per session were reduced.

3. There was increased reliance on student trainees to fill service gaps.

4. Initiation of services might simply be postponed until later in the

year, sometimes indefinitely. One speech specialist rationalized such delay by explaining that many speech difficulties were maturational; by the time they got to many of the children, their speech problems would have disappeared anyway.

5. Cost considerations were explicitly raised during the deliberations of core evaluation teams. One system, for example, maintained an informal quota for costly private school placements. A new child would not be placed until one had been returned from a private school, thereby theoretically opening up a slot. Speculation was frequently voiced in core evaluation team meetings, usually by administrators, about whether the school committee might balk at a particular payment for service.

6. Service needs voiced by parents during team meetings were not heard, particularly when the concern suggested the need for counseling for emotional problems. Mental health services were generally in short supply in the schools, and few school systems maintained the kind of relation with community mental health centers that would give their referrals priority treatment.

The problem of insufficient services has persisted. The special commision on Chapter 766 found:

Children [are sometimes] not being served although they have had a core evaluation, because appropriate service is not available.

Special education teachers and parents . . . have expressed a deficiency in full services: e.g., physical therapy, occupational therapy, speech and language, and counseling services for parents.

Services to special needs children in the regular classroom are not always adequate [and there is] a lack of support services.

At the secondary level programs and services are weak and inadequate to meet the needs of special education students.

Vocational and/or job training services are not widely available.

There is a lack of appropriate services for high-risk low-incidence populations currently in state hospitals.[43]

Elimination of Labeling

Section 1 of Chapter 766 sets forth the rationale for the elimination of labeling as follows:

The General Court further finds that past methods of labeling and defining needs of children have had a stigmatizing effect and have caused special education programs to be overly narrow and rigid, both in their content and their inclusion and exclusion policies.[44]

The remedy as prescribed by the law is to define

the needs of children requiring special education in a broad and flexible manner, leaving it to state agencies to provide more detailed definitions which recognize that such children have a variety of characteristics and needs.[45]

This provision, which carries the individualized approach to children with special needs a step beyond the federal law, has a curious history. Staff of the Joint Committee on Education were concerned about the multiplicity of designations for handicapped children and the overlapping and often conflicting provisions for them in state statutes. Their aim was to provide a codification of these measures through Chapter 766 and to leave it to the Department of Education to come up with a more logical and consistent set of labels.[46] However, parent and advocacy groups reflecting a sociological perspective were concerned about the effects of labels on the assessment and treatment of children. Their view prevailed. The requirement that the use of descriptive labels be discontinued conflicts with the needs of street-level bureaucracies to classify, sort, and differentially treat clients. Not only do labels function as client management aids, they also help define worker relationships to clients.

In Massachusetts there has been an official reduction in the use of labels at all levels and a definite shift to individual behavioral descriptions as required under the regulations. However, the use of labels persists, and new labels have been invented. The persistence of labels is perhaps best exemplified by the fact that the Division of Special Education, to comply with federal guidelines, still requires local systems to report, as they had in the past, the numbers and expenditures for mentally retarded, physically handicapped, partially seeing, speech-hearing handicapped, emotionally disturbed, and learning disabled children.[47]

The objective of eliminating labeling is only wishful thinking when individualized attention and services cannot be provided because of the need to process clients on a mass basis. It may be useful to clean up labels previously regarded as stigmatizing, but verbal sanitation does not in itself integrate children who used to be segregated. Since the school has to call them *something*, labeling persists in new forms.

Perhaps of greatest potential significance was the hope of special education reformers that the elimination of labeling would force school personnel to designate children individually by their potential for growth rather than by their deficits. However, this aspiration was often lost in the schools' desperate efforts to complete required assessment procedures, their lack of personnel relative to the new demands, and the absence of training for new responsibilities. What little training took place in Massachusetts was to instruct personnel in completing the new forms.

Despite the individualizing mainstreaming thrust of PL 94–142 and its emphasis on a "comprehensive system of personnel development," federal training priorities continue to support the categorical approach.[48] Most of the training money spent by the U.S. Bureau of Education for the Handicapped supports the university preparation of special educators; little is spent for in-service training of classroom teachers, even though "the majority of handicapped children spend all or most of their day in regular classrooms under the supervision of regular classroom teachers."[49] Specialist training for at least some categories is directed primarily toward preparing specialists to staff self-contained classes; there are virtually no federally funded pre- or in-service programs to help special educators develop the consulting skills necessary to support the regular class teacher's work with mainstreamed children.[50]

Under the circumstances teachers and individual specialists remain responsible for thinking as best they can about individual children. Special attention and individualized programming, if it is to be realized at all, has to be carved from the time available to discharge traditional multiple responsibilities, usually without the benefit of colleagues' help.

8
Humanizing Human Service Bureaucracies: Bureaucratic Reform or Client Control?

In implementing Chapter 766, Massachusetts schools confronted challenges to their management capabilities comparable to those now faced by all school systems under the federal special education reform law, PL 94–142, the Education for All Handicapped Children Act of 1975. They were obliged to identify all children requiring special education and support services, including those both younger and older than they had previously served. They were charged with administering a complex assessment and planning process employing a multidisciplinary team of specialists and involving parents to an unprecedented degree. They were made responsible for designing individualized programs and services for all students with special needs; if needed services did not exist within the schools, they were obliged to develop or purchase them through contract arrangements.

The school systems studied faced these requirements constrained by a lack of specific guidance from the Massachusetts Department of Education on how to meet them. They were told that their performance would be strictly monitored by the state, and they were subject to unofficial monitoring by parent and advocacy groups whom they considered hostile. Their early attempts to clarify their responsibilities were met with a confused response from a Division of Special Education staff, whom they considered biased against them. While they could expect to expend substantially increased amounts for special education, they could not know with certainty whether these costs would be reimbursed. School administrators found themselves caught between the requirements to comply with the law, which they took quite seriously, and the certainty that their school committees would at some point rebel against expenditures that would lead to substantially increased property taxes.

Special education personnel thus experienced pressures to accomplish enormous tasks in a short period of time with no certainty that resources would be substantially greater than those they had enjoyed before the new requirements were imposed. Many school systems had been moving in the direction indicated by 766, but now they *had* to accomplish what previously had been a matter of voluntary compliance with slowly changing professional practices. School personnel had to cope with their new job requirements in ways that would permit an acceptable solution to what appeared to be impossible demands.

That the school systems studied accomplished so much is a tribute to the dedication of school personnel. They engaged in extensive community outreach efforts to locate children with special needs who might otherwise have been unserved. They succeeded in processing hundreds of children and offering new and increased programs and services to them. They began involving parents in educational planning and opened up the decision-making process to contributions from a variety of professional perspectives. They attempted in many instances to modify their placement procedures to permit the implementation of individually designed education plans. Perhaps most important of all, in carrying out these measures they initiated a redress of the traditionally uneven balance between regular and special education programs, thereby giving special education a more prominent role.

However, in certain respects the new law, by dictating so much, actually dictated very little. Like police officers who are required to enforce so many regulations that they are effectively freed to enforce the law selectively, or public welfare workers who cannot master the encyclopedic and constantly changing eligibility requirements and so operate with a much smaller set of regulations, special education personnel had to contrive their own adjustments to the multiple demands they encountered.

School systems and individual schools within systems produced varied policies in their attempts to meet the new demands given the constraints of available resources. At the individual level, too, special education personnel varied in their responses. Among their varied ways of coping the following patterns could be observed.

They rationed (effectively placed limits on) the number of assessments they performed. They neglected to conduct assessments, placed limits on the numbers that were held, and biased the scheduling of assessment in favor of those who were behavior problems, were not likely to cost the systems money, or met the needs of school personnel who sought to exercise individual specialties.

To ration services, they reduced the hours of assignment, transferred children receiving individual treatment to group treatment settings, replaced instruction by more experienced and costly personnel with that of part-time tutors and students-in-training. They short-circuited bureaucratic requirements for completion of forms and procedures designed to protect the interests of children and parents. They minimized potentially time-consuming problems of client compliance through prior agreements on recommendations and by securing client deference to their "superior" judgment through manipulation of the symbols of professional authority. They sought to secure their work environment—individually, by referring (dumping) students who posed the greatest threat to classroom control or by recruiting students with whom they were trained to work; collectively, by seeking contractual agreements that the work load of the new law would not increase their overall responsibilities. While the pattern of responses among school systems and individual schools varied, there was a constant need to routinize, ration resources, control uncertainties, and define tasks in order to derive satisfactory solutions to the new demands.

In the aggregate these responses severely compromised the objectives of the law. This compromise occurred without any conscious intent to evade or sabotage implementation. On the contrary, school personnel, particularly those in front-line positions, were enthusiastic about the law's reform objectives and sincerely dedicated to their realization. This concern was evidenced in their extraordinary and sustained work effort, which went well beyond that required by their respective contracts. Yet paradoxically this effort resulted in the routinization of procedures intended to provide individualized initiatives.

This study demonstrates the policymaking role of street-level bureaucrats and supports the view that public schools recreate and reinforce the social class structure of the larger society. Radical critics of public education argue that advantaged social groups exert power to preserve preferential treatment for their children while children of the less advantaged get tracked to the bottom of the social hierarchy.[1] Thus social relations within the schools correspond to those within the society, and schools serve the existing social order "by developing lower-class children to be better workers and middle-class ones to be better managers in the corporate economy, and by reproducing the social relations of production in the schools to inculcate children with values and norms supportive of capitalistic work organization."[2]

In the past all children who needed special education have, as a class, made up a disadvantaged group, regardless of their individual family circumstances. Coincidentally their potential contribution to the economy has generally been undervalued. Federal and state reform legislation seeks to alter the treatment of all such children and improve their status in relation to children in the mainstream of regular education. The remedies prescribed by law are to apply to all children regardless of race, sex, economic status, or handicap. Federal law prescribes specific administrative procedures intended to provide equal protection for all handicapped children. Despite the legal requirements for equity, well-intended personnel are constrained by the circumstances of their work to respond differently to children and parents who have similar needs. The insufficiency of resources requires that educational benefits be distributed unevenly; the existing structure of social relations and the uneven distribution of resources and bureaucratic competence among clients—children and parents—serves to bias the responses of the school personnel in favor of the more affluent. This biasing does not occur deliberately. Most of the school personnel I observed and interviewed would be shocked at the suggestion that they favored the children of middle-class and affluent parents over those of the poor. Most, I believe, would express strong agreement with the proposition that *all* children should be treated alike, regardless of race or income or professional status of their parents. Yet when forced to discriminate among clients because of the need to conserve resources, these same well-intentioned personnel would respond more generously to those of higher socioeconomic status, who also had the greatest potential to challenge their decisions.

While the plight of poor and minority children being shunted to inferior special classes helped generate the support necessary to pass reform legislation, these children have benefited the least. Even without any overt discrimination by individual school personnel, children of the poor and minorities fare worse despite procedural safeguards ostensibly intended to prevent discriminatory treatment.

The routinization of responses to legal requirements affects all children to some extent but falls most heavily on the poor. Where informal priorities must be exerted and supposedly universal public benefits rationed, the poor are likely to benefit less than the more advantaged. On the whole, poor and minority children are still more likely to be assigned the more stigmatizing "mentally retarded" label than the more socially acceptable designation of "learning disabled," even while exhibiting the same constellation of strengths and deficits. When exhibiting behavioral problems, they are more likely to be tracked into underfinanced and inferior public programs, while children of the affluent are sent to higher-quality private schools at public expense.[3] Safeguards ostensibly available for all children and parents serve the interests of the middle class and affluent far better than the poor. Provisions for advocates and for appeals from school decisions provide the illusion of procedural fairness, but the almost exclusive use of these mechanisms by the more affluent parents demonstrates that this fairness works more for the rich than the poor.

The patterns of differential response to children of the rich and middle class and children of the poor are reinforced by residential patterns of social stratification. The more affluent school systems provide more and better special education services. The relative advantages of schools in more affluent communities are reinforced by their superior ability to attract highly qualified staff and competent leadership. This relative staff advantage places such school systems in a superior position to secure state and federal discretionary grants and to manipulate financial and program reports to obtain a greater share of available funds under state reimbursement formulas. In Massachusetts the so-called equalizing formula for education reimbursements actually increased the resource disparities between rich and poor systems for both regular and special education.

Individually and in organized advocacy groups, parents in the more affluent communities are better able to press for preferred treatment for their children through the use of established appeals machinery, support by professional and lay advocates, political pressure on school board members, legislators, and administrators, and through the threat of court action. In their interactions with school personnel, they are treated more deferentially and are consequently more likely to be heard by education plan team members. Thus a "universalistic" policy implanted in a service bureaucracy that itself reflects and reproduces particularistic social divisions necessarily produces biased outcomes.

What are the implications of these findings? Front-line personnel, street-level bureaucrats as I have called them, unintentionally but effectively "make" policy through their responses to the multiple demands placed on them. This street-level policy delivered to the public is at variance with formal or official policy reflected in law, regulations, and procedures. And without any conscious wish to do so, the street-level bureaucrats, as they strive to cope with the demands of their jobs, bias the delivery of public benefits in favor of the more affluent.

This study, in drawing attention to specific problems in the implementation of special education reform, suggests at least by implication a number of administrative remedies. Improved data and accounting systems at the state and local levels, improved training and orientation programs for regular and special education personnel, better preparation of education plan team members, the provision of more and improved technical assistance to localities, increased support of mediation and advocacy programs, and other administrative measures could improve services for more children. Such administrative solutions should be pursued; yet it would be fatuous to assume that administrative measures alone can "solve" many of the problems that plague special education reform efforts. The solutions to many of the problems may not be obvious or at least debatable. For example, some maintain that investment in in-service training for regular class teachers is not as cost-effective as the alternative strategy of training specialists. More basically, there continues to be debate over the concept of mainstreaming; some fear that children will be placed in regular classes without sufficient preparation or support and that they may suffer as a result. Segregation of children needing special education, a practice that today has been called into question, was a major innovation in the 1920s. Today's solutions all too often become tomorrow's problems.

The provision of specialist services can engender a fragmented response to children and diffuse responsibility for service provision. Procedures intended to increase accountability bury personnel in paperwork and thereby contribute to the routinization of assessment and rationing of services. Even the provision of additional funds can distort priorities, lead to the overzealous placement of children in overly restrictive settings, and further exacerbate disparities between rich and poor districts.

Other problems remain beyond the purview of the educational establishment. The overall inadequacy and fragmentation of supportive human service programs provided through a maze of state, federal, and local agencies under public, voluntary, and private auspices contribute to the burden borne by the schools.

In pointing out the complexities and sometimes perverse consequences of certain administrative remedies, I do not wish to suggest that they not be attempted. Many improvements may be introduced at all administrative levels. The nature of specific remedies will become even more apparent as state and localities accumulate experience in meeting the provisions of PL 94-142. In this regard the U.S. Bureau of Education for the Handicapped has initiated a research and evaluation strategy that, through the funding of small narrowly focused case studies, will yield information on specific implementation problems; this information should in turn suggest administrative steps to correct these problems. Concurrently BEH has also supported the identification and development of exemplary special education and IEP administrative program models, and they have undertaken to disseminate pertinent material to aid state and local education agencies in mounting programs.

Let us not deceive ourselves, however, into thinking that administrative remedies, no matter how well planned or executed, will suffice in correcting or preventing the kinds of bias that this study has identified. There are limits to the efficacy of administrative reform. Procedural reforms to engender client participation, safeguard client rights, and facilitate individualized consideration by human service bureaucracies may be little more than symbolic unless buttressed by policies and resources sufficient to make them work. Street-level bureaucrats cannot treat clients as individuals unless they have sufficient time to interact with them individually. Due process mechanisms are meaningful to clients only to the extent that clients possess sufficient resources to use them. The arbitrary sorting of clients may be minimized only to the extent that assessment teams have sufficient time, are carefully trained, their deliberations monitored, and the range of possible responses broadened to include interventions to modify the bureaucracy's impact on clients.

Many of the problems in implementing special education reform are attributable to the failure of federal and state legislative bodies to provide funds commensurate with the scope of responsibilities assigned to the schools. Massachusetts school systems faced legal requirements to provide expensive new services to increased numbers of students without increased state support. The federal law contains a sharply escalating funding authorization, but initial appropriations have already fallen short of the authorized amounts.

The job-coping behaviors of street-level bureaucrats are related to the level of resources. In this sense the systematic undermining of policies to promote individualization of services to clients is abetted by resource constraints. Most conceivable administrative improvements require some minimum of resources.

These problems are not simply due to insufficient funds; however, there can be few solutions without more money. It is unlikely that the Massachusetts or federal special education reform laws could have been adopted if the legislatures had been forced to deal realistically with the resource issues. It remains unlikely that failures in realizing reform objectives will now goad these same legislative bodies into finding the necessary resources. One must therefore question the effect of social legislation that sets forth patently unattainable objectives.

It may be argued that this analysis is overly harsh. Special education reform legislation has in fact shifted educational priorities and has resulted in increased and better services for many children. For example, one school system studied, although plagued by many of the problems discussed, and lacking in scope of coverage, nonetheless operated a qualitatively superior program.

One can argue persuasively that state and federal laws require immediate compliance but that the complexities of organizational change and fiscal realities constrain implementation, so that compliance can be achieved only over a period of years. In studying the early responses of school systems to new requirements, one would necessarily find deficiencies that will take time to correct. Although the law establishes standards toward which all may strive, some school systems will necessarily achieve them sooner than others.

Michael Kirst has advanced such an argument with regard to Title I of the Elementary and Secondary Education Act.[4] Some analysts point to this legislation as demonstrating the barriers to achieving federal education policy objectives—in this instance, compensatory education for disadvantaged children—through legislation, even when accompanied by substantial federal funding.[5] Kirst maintains that significant advances have been achieved under ESEA Title I. Since these achievements have been evolutionary, however, they have escaped the notice of policy analysts who lack historical perspective. Interest group pressure, court challenges, and federal audits, Kirst argues, have resulted in numerous gradual changes over the years that cumulatively have been dramatic in directing funds to disadvantaged children.

Along these same lines, some have argued that special education reform objectives will take at least a decade to achieve and that we must look to incremental rather than immediate and widespread improvements. Indeed it is hard to imagine that special education programs will not improve over time, particularly in response to federal initiatives. In some localities services are presently nonexistent or else so poor that logic dictates that conditions must improve. At issue, however, is how much improvement for which children and how soon. The law requires an immediate response, and for good reason. Like other civil rights legislation, PL 94–142 and Section 504 of the Vocational Rehabilitation Act of 1973 were adopted to correct past discriminatory practices and to extend to the handicapped constitutional guarantees not previously available to them. It obviously will not, nor should not, satisfy handicapped children and their parents to suggest that they wait ten years to enjoy programs and services that by law they should have now.

Nor will the time-saving routines invoked by harried school

personnel simply wither away. There is no evidence that this has occurred in Massachusetts since the schools began in 1974 to implement that state's special education reform law. The initial press of referrals and assessments has not subsided. If it ever does, there will be reevaluations to catch up with. But perhaps even more significant is the likelihood that the routinization of procedures, once established, will persist. From the perspective of the street-level bureaucrat, it is easier and more economical to continue familiar routines than to develop new and more time-consuming work habits. In the life of organizations, traditions once established are difficult to change.

Furthermore, incentives for schools favor the routinization of child processing mechanisms. The federal law, like Massachusetts law, at the same time requires and rewards the identification and assessment of children in need of special education. No reimbursements may be claimed for children until *after* the assessment and education program development process has been completed for them. However, there are no comparable incentives for the development of high-quality services. In fact, schools will maximize resources under PL 94–142 by identifying and conducting education plan meetings for as many children as possible up to the 12 percent of enrollment ceiling, but serving them as cheaply as they can. Educational leadership, professional pride, and parent pressure may intervene to produce highly individualized, richly staffed, and high-quality special education programs, particularly in communities with sufficient wealth to pay for them. For school systems without these relative advantages, however, the outcome is likely to be assembly line assessments and minimal service options.

That legal requirements exceed the current capacity and available resources of most school systems gives license to states and localities to comply selectively. They cannot, some will argue, be expected to accomplish the impossible. Furthermore the costs of noncompliance are not likely to be great. Enforcement responsibilities have been assigned to the Department of Health, Education, and Welfare's Office for Civil Rights; its record of enforcement of civil rights law has been questioned, and it currently faces a three-year backlog of complaints. Although HEW has the authority to withhold funds in instances of noncompliance, the experience with similar legislation and the reality of state-federal relations suggest that this authority will be exercised only in rare and extreme cases.

In many respects the case of special education illustrates the limits of efforts to improve the situation of disadvantaged groups solely through bureaucratic interventions. Since the passage of the Social Security Act, which marked the beginning in this country of the modern welfare state, more and more citizens have become dependent on public bureaucracies to supply the basic necessities of life. The insufficiency of the market system to satisfy basic needs has led to the development and enlargement of public service bureaucracies. Increasing numbers have had to look to public bureaucracies to assure economic security, provide health services, housing, food, jobs, and help with problems of adjustment.

Bureaucracies provide a relatively efficient means of meeting need on a massive scale, but this efficiency is achieved at some cost. Human service bureaucracies must by their very nature make distinctions among clients, determine eligibility for service, direct clients to appropriate services, monitor their progress, and categorize and organize services to reflect specialization. In our terms clients are classified, sorted, and routed to bureaucratic subunits, then slotted into available service categories. Organizational efficiency is maximized through the rationing of access to service and the routinization of procedures to facilitate the entry, passage, and exit of clients.

There is a tension between the organizational imperatives requisite to the mass processing of clients and the treatment of clients in a manner that shows respect for individual differences among them. Human service bureaucracies attempt to resolve this tension by delegating discretionary authority to front-line staff. One constraint to the arbitrary exercise of this authority is the recruitment of professional or semiprofessional staff whose prior socialization or training provides them with a generally shared set of values, standards, and intervention skills. Their work is also circumscribed by rules and procedures that limit their exercise of discretion.

The processing of clients on a mass basis inevitably requires that organizations regulate or control clients' interactions with organizational representatives. Without such control there is no organization, only chaos. The problem that human service bureaucracies must address in planning encounters with clients is to determine how much and what kind of control of client access and passage through the organization is needed.

Techniques of systems analysis may aid administrators in planning and monitoring the processing of clients or, more accurately, tracking the paperwork that in many respects represents the client to the organization. However, much of what actually happens to clients is determined by the individual work adaptations of frontline personnel which, when taken together, make up the "underlife" of the organization.[6] The individualization of interactions with clients is not and cannot be an absolute; it is a matter of degree. Reforms that seek to "humanize" bureaucracies—to engender a more personal, warm, supportive, flexible, and individual relationship between bureaucratic functionaries and their clients—at some point run up against both manifest and latent organizational requirements to control client behavior in order to facilitate their processing. Consequently administrative reform efforts may sometimes be more symbolic than real and may simply result in more subtle, less visible means of controlling clients while preserving the illusion of humanizing reform.

In the case of special education reform policies, parents are "involved" but not heard; children are no longer dumped into special classes but are referred to "resource rooms" and specialists, sometimes with exclusionary intent; multidisciplinary planning teams are assembled, but decisions still reflect single standardized test scores or the will of dominant team members; "individualized" education plans for each child are written but are copied from standard formats or from previously developed plans; services are planned but not provided.

Such subterfuge would break down entirely if uniformly and invariably invoked. It is therefore important that sufficient exceptions be made so that all might believe that the reform procedures are working to some extent. But exceptions are usually made for those whose status gains them favored treatment or who pose the greatest threat to the organizational routine.

It is convenient but deceptive to think of the failure of human service bureaucracies to consistently and uniformly provide humane individualized treatment of clients as simply reflecting shortcomings in administration or in implementation.[7] To do so focuses responsibility on the bureaucracies and their staff for problems that remain beyond their capacities to correct.

It is the function of such bureaucracies to treat or serve individuals; the social conditions that may be responsible for the problems of clients remain well beyond their purview.[8] In fact, the provision of even inadequate services serves to pacify potentially rebellious elements and satisfies our collective sense of justice and humanity, while leaving unexamined and undisturbed the inequities in existing patterns of social relations.[9]

Human service bureaucracies and those who work within them are also convenient scapegoats for the collective insufficiencies of human service programs. They are much maligned as impersonal, unfeeling, wasteful, inefficient, rigid, inflexible. At the same time, they are underfinanced, overcontrolled, fragmented, and assigned impossible tasks. Their failures demonstrate the futility of applying administrative remedies to political problems.

The problems that led to special education reform legislation were essentially political; they were problems of unequal distribution of public benefits. Certain children were arbitrarily excluded from public education or denied services and programs simply on the basis of a handicapping condition, although other factors such as race and socioeconomic status were sometimes involved. The passage of reform legislation at the persistent instigation of parent, advocacy, and civil rights groups served to accommodate the demands of these groups and provide symbolic reassurance to the public of a governmental commitment and concern for the needs of a group disadvantaged through no fault of its own. To continue to deny or ignore the legitimate demands of this group would have constituted a gross violation of humanistic principles that we as a nation like to believe we adhere to.[10] The failure to appropriate sufficient funds to fully implement the law and its imposition on a public education infrastructure characterized by vast disparities in resources and capabilities and facing a general erosion of financial support virtually guarantees the kind of "implementation" problems encountered in this study. In a broader sense the persistent inattention to problems of inequality also guarantees unequal treatment of citizens and unequal distribution of public benefits by public bureaucracies, including schools. Such problems cannot be "solved" administratively.

In one sense special education laws fit well within the tradition of reform legislation that seeks to improve the situation of disadvantaged groups or soften the impact on them of bureaucratic encounters. This is a tradition where lofty objectives are espoused, but minimal resources committed. The failures that ensue are deemed failures in implementation.

The reform agenda of the past two decades offers numerous examples. The antipoverty programs of the 1960s introduced many innovative departures to assist the poor, including broad "institutional change" strategies to modify, bypass, or coordinate human service bureaucracies that delivered services to the poor; the employment of paraprofessionals to increase employment opportunities for the poor and at the same time increase the capacity of the employing bureaucracies to communicate with their clients; and requirements for participation of the poor in the planning and oversight of programs affecting them. Insensitive bureaucracies were defined as part of the problem, and the anger and frustration of the poor were directed against them.

Other antipoverty strategies included the provision of social services and job training programs that focused attention on the alleged deficits of the poor themselves. Meanwhile the underlying causes of poverty remained unexamined and unaffected.

To the extent that local community action agencies succeeded in challenging control over local services by entrenched political elites, they were discredited and eventually faced curtailment of their financial support. At the same time paraprofessionals and poverty representatives were co-opted, and the more desirable public jobs and training opportunities allocated to the more advantaged of the poor. The war on poverty was fought with resources and tactics sufficient only for a brief skirmish preceding what has become a major retreat.

More recent reform measures have also helped to preserve the illusion of progressive improvement in our treatment of disadvantaged groups while merely shifting the locale of their suffering. A case in point is the current trend toward deinstitutionalization of deviant populations—the developmentally disabled, mentally ill, and juvenile and status offenders. The removal of portions of these populations from institutions offers the politically attractive prospect of carrying out a progressive reform measure while conserving resources. The community-based support services essential to the success of such a strategy, however, are rarely provided on more than a token basis, and public attitudes defining such populations as deviant, nonproductive, and requiring isolation remain unaffected. The result is symbolized by the ex-mental patient ghettos now to be found in many of our large cities where residents are prey to exploitive landlords and merchants and street criminals.

The national system of community mental health centers, an essential adjunct to a deinstitutionalization strategy, is being gradually but effectively decimated as their federal "start-up" staffing grants expire. The convenient fiction is that localities will pick up the operating costs for these centers. Instead the centers are forced to assume even greater service responsibilities while facing a declining resource base.

Volunteer-initiated programs to assist victims of child abuse, rape, and incest or to provide shelters for battered women are lauded as demonstrating the vitality of the voluntary sector in responding quickly to emergent problems. Yet such programs must compete with others for a share of the declining resources, and the underlying social conditions that contribute to these problems remain unaffected.

The social program emphasis of the 1970s is well suited to the preservation of existing patterns of social stratification and avoids overburdening a stagnating economy.[11] The "new federalism" initiated by the Nixon administration has provided a convenient vehicle for the retreat from federal responsibility for addressing social problems by shifting decision making about program priorities to local elites. The result has been the diminution of social services, housing, and community development benefits for the poor and a reallocation of federal funds to the general support of local government.

The analysis in chapter 1 began with a discussion of the recent attention to problems of policy implementation. This study is itself an example of this emergent tradition of inquiry. The interest in implementation arose out of disillusionment with the failure of the social programs of the 1960s and concern about the perverse side effects often accompanying them. The lesson seemed to be that the passage of legislation was in itself insufficient to achieve social objectives and that therefore attention needed to be directed toward examining the conditions under which legislated policies were implemented. This reasoning seems logical and straightforward enough, but it is also based on the assumption, not sufficiently examined, that policy "failures" are administrative in nature and therefore amenable to administrative solutions. It is an interesting coincidence that the study of implementation should gain the attention of policy analysts in a time of general economic decline and retreat from attacks, even rhetorical, on major social problems.

There is a danger that the focus on policy implementation may itself contribute to this retreat by assigning responsibility for policy failures to the implementing bureaucracies and by emphasizing technological and administrative solutions that leave undisturbed existing social and economic inequalities. At a time when continuing economic decline threatens to heighten competition over shrinking resources, we must prepare to look beyond implementation to more fundamental solutions.

Notes

Chapter 1

1
Section 504 of the Rehabilitation Act of 1973, 29 U.S. Code 706, provides that "no otherwise qualified handicapped individual . . . shall, solely by reason of his handicap, be excluded from the participation in, be denied the benefits of, or be subjected to discrimination under any program or activity receiving federal financial assistance." "Rules and Regulations," Department of Health, Education, and Welfare, *Federal Register* 42:86 (May 4, 1977), part 4, p. 22676.

2
National School Public Relations Association, *Educating All the Handicapped* (Arlington, Va., 1977), p. 8.

3
J. S. Kakalik, "Policy Issues in Cost and Finance of Special Education," WN-9680-HEW mimeo (Santa Monica, Calif.: Rand Corporation, 1977), p. vii.

4
The summary of the law is based on PL 94-142, 94th Congress, Session 6, November 29, 1975, and the "Rules and Regulations," Department of Health, Education, and Welfare, Education of Handicapped Children, Implementation of Part B of the Education of the Handicapped Act, *Federal Register* 42:163 (August 23, 1977).

5
William H. Wilken and David O. Porter, "State Aid for Special Education—Who Benefits?" National Foundation for the Improvement of Education and the National Conference of State Legislatures, Washington, D.C., May 31, 1976, p. I-2.

6
Educating All the Handicapped, p. 17.

7
Wilken and Porter, p. III-27.

8
Commonwealth of Massachusetts, House No. 6429, "Second Interim Report of the Special Commission Relative to the Laws of the Commonwealth Pertaining to Elementary and Secondary Education as They Relate to Unequal Educational Opportunity and Services," August 10, 1977, pp. 10, 19.

9
For relatively early discussions of the importance of examining policy "outcomes" and the distribution of public benefits see, for example, Herbert Jacob and Michael Lipsky, "Outputs, Structure and Power: An Assessment of Changes in the Study of State and Local Politics," *Journal of Politics* 30 (May 1968): 510-538. See also the discussion in Frank Levy, Arnold

Meltsner, and Aaron Wildavsky, *Urban Outcomes* (Berkeley, Calif.: University of California Press, 1974).

10

See Murray Edelman, *The Symbolic Uses of Politics* (Champaign, Ill.: University of Illinois Press, 1964), and his *Political Language: Words That Succeed and Policies That Fail* (New York: Academic Press, 1977), and Theodore Lowi, *The End of Liberalism* (New York: Norton, 1969).

11

Recent works dealing with the implementation process include Eugene Bardach, *The Implementation Game* (Cambridge, Mass: MIT Press, 1977), and Jeffrey Pressman and Aaron Wildavsky, *Implementation* (Berkeley, Calif.: University of California Press, 1973). See also Martha Derthick, *New Towns In-Town* (Washington, D.C.: Urban Institute, 1972); Jerome Murphy, *State Education Agencies and Discretionary Funds* (Lexington, Mass.: D.C. Heath, 1974); Jerome Murphy, "Title I of ESEA: The Politics of Implementing Federal Education Reform," *Harvard Educational Review* 41 (February 1971): 35–63; Lowi, *End of Liberalism.*

Numerous treatises on specific federal policies [for example, Bernard Frieden and Marshall Kaplan, *The Politics of Neglect* (Cambridge, Mass.: MIT Press, 1975) or Daniel P. Moynihan, *Maximum Feasible Misunderstanding* (New York: Free Press, 1969)], describe the fate of policy from conception through passage to implementation and provide material for studies of implementation from the perspective of new federal initiatives. This literature is reviewed and commented on in the following general discussions: Donald Van Meter and Carl Van Horn, "The Policy Implementation Process: A Conceptual Framework," *Administration and Society* 6 (November 1974): 445–488; Walter Williams, ed., "Special Issue on Implementation," *Policy Analysis* 1 (Summer 1975); Erwin C. Hargrove, *The Missing Link: The Study of the Implementation of Social Policy* (Washington, D.C.: The Urban Institute, 1975).

12

Hargrove puts it this way: "The academic political scientists . . . begin with a policy as it was initially shaped by the politics of reaching agreement and then chart the continuing politics of program administration in which politicians, bureaucrats, interest groups and publics vie for control over the direction of the program" (*The Missing Link*, p. 3).

13

An elaboration of this formulation may be found in Michael Lipsky, "Toward a Theory of Street-Level Bureaucracy," in Willis Hawley and Michael Lipsky, eds., *Theoretical Perspectives on Urban Politics* (Englewood Cliffs, N.J.: Prentice Hall, 1976), pp. 186–212.

For examples of studies employing the street-level bureaucracy perspective, see Jeffrey Prottas, "The Power of the Street-Level Bureaucrat in

Public Service Bureaucracies," *Urban Affairs Quarterly* 13 (March 1978): 285–313, and Carl J. Hosticka, "Street-Level Bureaucrats' Encounters with Clients: Cases from the Justice System" (Paper presented at the American Society of Public Administration National Conference, Chicago, April 1975; mimeographed).

14
Anthony Downs discusses the demand for free goods and the consequent need for bureaucracies to place "costs" on them in *Inside Bureaucracy* (Boston: Little, Brown and Co. 1967), p. 188.

15
The causes and effects of job burnout are discussed in Christina Maslach, "How People Cope," and Robert Kahn, "Prevention and Remedies," *Public Welfare* 36 (Spring 1978) pp. 56–58, 61–63.

16
See Amitai Etzioni, ed., *The Semi-Professions and Their Organization* (New York: Free Press, 1969). Whether street-level bureaucrats are professionals is a significant question with implications for the extent to which the society fully or only partially grants them autonomy in their work. Street-level bureaucrats act with sanctioned discretion like professionals (and some, such as legal services attorneys, clearly must be regarded as professionals), but they are sometimes subject to close supervision as well.

17
In popular use the word *policy* sometimes refers to official intentions; at other times it refers to what actually happens. Attempting to incorporate both meanings into their definition, Pressman and Wildavsky use the word policy to designate a more or less implicit hypothesis about what will happen if certain specified actions are taken. (If money is spent to retrain people, some of them will obtain jobs. *Implementation*, pp. xi–xvii.)

I will sometimes use the word policy in this sense, intending to refer to the intentions and the theory of people who make a decision to act under the color of law (a statute, an executive order, a judicial decree). At other times, when I am discussing the interaction between the activities of lower-level administrators and workers and the results they produce on behalf of the government, I use the word to designate what actually happens. This dual usage is consistent with common usage; and as in common usage, I trust that the context of the discussion will make the meaning clear. For another review of the meanings of the terms policy and implementation see Hargrove, *The Missing Link*, pp. 1–14.

18
The policymaking role of street-level bureaucrats is discussed in Michael Lipsky, "Standing the Study of Policy Implementation on Its Head," in *American Politics and Public Policy*, ed. Martha Weinberg and W. Dean Burnham (Cambridge, Mass.: MIT Press, 1978).

Peter Blau, in *The Dynamics of Bureaucracy* (Chicago: University of Chicago Press, 1955), pp. 36–56, provides something of a model for this approach when he reports the ways in which changes in measurements of success altered the priorities of employment counselors. Many sociological works focusing on occupational and work structure are useful from this perspective, although they rarely focus on changes in official policy. See, for example, Julius A. Roth, "Some Contingencies of the Moral Evaluation and Control of Clientele: The Case of the Hospital Emergency Service," *American Journal of Sociology* 77 (March 1972): 839–856; Howard S. Becker, "The Teacher in the Authority System of the Public School," *Journal of Educational Sociology* 27 (November 1953): 128–141.

19
Downs, *Inside Bureaucracy*, p. 111.

20
Kakalik, "Policy Issues," p. 58.

21
These disparities are documented in the following works: James S. Kakalik et al., *Services for Handicapped Youth* (Santa Monica, Calif.: Rand, 1974); Wilken and Porter, "State Aid for Special Education"; William H. Wilken and John J. Callahan, "Disparities in Special Education Services: The Need for Better Fiscal Management," Legislators' Education Action Project, National Conference of State Legislatures, Washington, D.C., August 31, 1976; National School Public Relations Association, *Educating All the Handicapped* (Arlington, Va., 1977); "BEH Data Notes," Bureau of Education for the Handicapped, U.S. Department of Health, Education, and Welfare, September 1977; Commonwealth of Massachusetts, House No. 6429, "Second Interim Report Pertaining to Unequal Educational Opportunity"; David M. Sheehan, "The Children's Puzzle: A Study of Services to Children in Massachusetts," Report to the House Ways and Means Committee, Institute for Governmental Services, University of Massachusetts, Boston, February 1977.

22
Wilken and Callahan, "Disparities," pp. 15, 17.

23
Ibid., p. 3; also Sheehan, "The Children's Puzzle," esp. pp. 4–8.

24
William H. Donaldson, "Community Profiles and Special Education Funding Impact," Internal Memorandum, Massachusetts Department of Education, Division of Special Education, Bureau of Management, March 1977.

25
Ibid., p. 5.

26
Ibid., p. 4

27
Educating All the Handicapped, pp. 41–43.

28
Wilken and Callahan, "Disparities," p. 11.

29
Sheehan, "The Children's Puzzle," p. 7. This finding is also reported by Wilken and Callahan in "Disparities," p. 25.

30
Commonwealth of Massachusetts, House No. 6429, "Second Interim Report Pertaining to Unequal Educational Opportunity," p. 14.

31
Milton Budoff, Sibyl Mitchell, and Lawrence Kotin, "Procedural Due Process: Its Application to Special Education and Its Implications for Teacher Training" (Cambridge, Mass.: Research Institute for Educational Problems, August 1976); Lawrence Kotin and Nancy Eager, "Due Process in Special Education: A Legal Analysis" (Cambridge, Mass.: Research Institute for Educational Problems, February 1977).

32
Stephen J. Apter, "Implications of Ecological Theory: Toward a Community Special Education Model," *Exceptional Children* 43 (March 1977): 366–373; Nicholas Hobbs, *The Futures of Children: Categories, Labels, and Their Consequences* (San Francisco: Jossey-Bass, 1975).

33
William Ryan, *Blaming the Victim* (New York: Vintage Books, 1971).

Chapter 2

1
For an excellent general summary of concerns leading to the passage of PL 94-142, see Alan Abeson and Jeffrey Zettel, "The End of the Quiet Revolution: The Education for All Handicapped Children Act of 1975," *Exceptional Children* 44 (October 1977): 115–128.

2
See, for example, Orville G. Johnson, "Special Education for the Mentally Handicapped—A Paradox," *Exceptional Children* 29 (October 1962): 62–69; Howard L. Sparks and Leonard S. Blackman, "What Is Special about Special Education Revisited: The Mentally Retarded," *Exceptional Children* 31 (January 1965): 242–247; Lloyd M. Dunn, "Special Education for the Mildly Retarded—Is Much of It Justifiable?" *Exceptional Children* 35 (September 1968): 5–22; Stephen M. Lilly, "Special Education: A Teapot in a Tempest," *Exceptional Children* 37 (September 1970): 43–49.

A cautionary viewpoint is presented by James O. Smith and Joan R. Arkans, who argue for retention of special classes for the "lower measured intellectual level retarded children" in "Now More Than Ever: A Case for the Special Class," *Exceptional Children* 40 (April 1974): 497–502.

For an early summary of parent-instigated court challenges to testing, placement procedures, and special class programming, see Sterling L. Ross, Jr., et al., "Confrontation: Special Education Placement and the Law," *Exceptional Children* (September 1971): 5–12.

3
Johnson, "Special Education," p. 66.

4
Task Force on Children Out of School, *The Way We Go to School: The Exclusion of Children in Boston* (Boston: Beacon Press, 1971), pp. 49, 56.

5
Burton Blatt and Frank Garfunkel, "Massachusetts Study of Educational Opportunities for Handicapped and Disadvantaged Children," Massachusetts Advisory Council on Education, January 1971, pp. 6–9 (henceforth referred to as the MACE report). The MACE report, together with an earlier evaluation of the state's Chapter 750 program for the education of mentally retarded children (Herbert J. Hoffman, Massachusetts Advisory Council on Education, *Take A Giant Step*, Boston, 1970) and the 1971 publication of *The Way We Go to School* contributed directly to the passage of Chapter 766. The three reports provided a clear indictment of current special education practices and offered specific recommendations for change.

6
These developments are described in Lloyd E. Ohlin, Alden D. Miller, and Robert B. Coates, *Juvenile Correction Reform in Massachusetts: A Preliminary Report of the Center for Criminal Justice of the Harvard Law School* (Washington, D.C.. U.S. Government Printing Office, 1977); and Howard W. Polsky and Yitzhak Bacal, *Correctional Youth Reform: The Massachusetts Experience* (Lexington, Mass.: Lexington Books, 1978). See also Lloyd E. Ohlin et al., "Radical Correction Reform: A Case Study of the Massachusetts Youth Correctional System," *Harvard Educational Review* 44 (February 1974): 74–111.

7
For a detailed treatment of school classification from a legal perspective, see David L. Kirp, "Schools as Sorters: The Constitutional and Policy Implications of Student Classification," *University of Pennsylvania Law Review* 121 (April 1973): 705–797; and Nicholas Hobbs, *The Future of Children: Categories, Labels, and Their Consequences* (San Francisco, Calif.: Jossey-Bass, 1975).

8
James S. Kakalik, "Policy Issues in Cost and Finance of Special Education,"

WN-980-HEW mimeo (Santa Monica, Calif.: Rand Corporation, March 1977), esp. pp. 9-11.

9

William H. Wilken and David O. Porter, "State Aid for Special Education: Who Benefits?" National Foundation for the Improvement of Education and the National Conference of State Legislatures, Washington, D.C., May 31, 1976, p. I-6.

10

National School Public Relations Association, *Educating All the Handicapped* (Arlington, Va.: 1977), p. 72.

11

Tom B. Gillung and Chauncy R. Rucker, "Labels and Teacher Expectations, *Exceptional Children* 43 (April 1977): 464-465.

12

MACE report, pp. 273-284.

13

Ibid., pp. 275-276.

14

Hoffman, *Take A Giant Step; The Way We Go to School*; MACE report.

15

According to its author, Lawrence Kotin, this statute was based on a Connecticut law and a model statute developed by the Council for Exceptional Children. Kotin was then serving with the State Commission on the Education of the Handicapped, and he subsequently served as a legal consultant to the Division of Special Education (personal interview, September 8, 1975).

16

William H. Creighton, "Chapter 766: An Overview," Undergraduate honors paper, Harvard University, Cambridge, Mass.: May 1974.

17

MACE report, p. 9.

18

Creighton, "Chapter 766," p. 14.

19

Robert Crabtree, former research director, Joint Committee on Education, described the lobbying effort as "a staff operation" (interview, April 28, 1975).

20

Creighton, "Chapter 766," pp. 14-16.

21

Ibid., p. 21 It is likely that the PL 94-142 funding formula was designed to achieve the same objective. The initial authorization starts at a very low level and reaches full funding after five years. The National School Public Relations Association (*Educating All the Handicapped*, p. 14) suggests the following rationale for this formula:

Good political sense probably dictated it. It would be very hard to get Congress to accept a new program starting out with a $3 billion per year price tag. But a $300 million authorization apparently didn't sound too bad. Supporters of the law are counting on educators—hardpressed to meet the law's requirements—to pressure Congress to come up with extra funding in succeeding years.

22

"Bartley Halts Special Education Debate," *Boston Globe*, May 23, 1974.

23

Milton Budoff, "Engendering Change in Special Education Practices," *Harvard Educational Review* 45 (November 1975): 512.

24

David Kirp et al., "Legal Reform of Special Education: Empirical Studies and Procedural Proposals," *California Law Review* 62 (January 1974): 40–155. Kirp argues, however, that the procedural changes brought about through *PARC* v. *Commonwealth of Pennsylvania* did not in themselves result in altered practices in the schools.

25

Creighton, "Chapter 766," p. 19.

26

The Sargent bill was also drafted by Lawrence Kotin, who had drafted the MACE model statute on which Chapter 766 was based.

27

This assessment is supported by interviews held with a number of school administrators at the beginning of the 1974–75 school year. One special education administrator, in a memorandum to his superintendent, stated, "Indeed, much of what is good in Chapter 766 has long been standard practice in [our town] and elsewhere—not infrequently in the teeth of opposition from the state, which today mandates what yesterday it forbade."

Later in the year many administrators acknowledged that the law had in fact altered in positive ways their processing of children with special needs.

28

Interview with Fred Andleman, director of professional development, Massachusetts Teachers Association, April 9, 1975.

29

As Martha Derthick has observed, the lack of constituent interest in or need for a proposed program can be a source of implementation difficulty not always appreciated by legislators. In *New Towns In-Town* (Washington,

D.C.: Urban Institute, 1972) she documents the case of a presidentially inspired housing program that fell flat, in part due to a lack of interest and support from intended beneficiaries at the local level. No one had thought to ask whether the type of housing proposed was actually wanted.

30
The normal give-and-take of the legislative process can result in compromises that undermine the original intent of the legislation; or the legislative intent may be unrealistic or unattainable in any case. Edward C. Banfield, for example, shows how the Model Cities program was doomed through legislative compromise that transformed a large-scale demonstration project for several big cities into a more limited aid program for a great many localities. See his "Making a New Federal Program: Model Cities, 1964–68," in *Policy and Politics in America*, ed. Allan P. Sindler (Boston: Little, Brown and Co., 1973), pp. 124–158.

The growing tendency of legislatures to sidestep difficult implementation issues by writing vague, general laws in the hope that the details may be later worked out by the affected interest groups has been decried by Theodore Lowi in his critique of interest group liberalism, *The End of Liberalism* (New York: Norton, 1969).

In the case of Chapter 766 and PL 94–142, the relevant interest groups engaged in intensive bargaining *before* passage of the law and during the writing of the regulations. The result was specificity in both the law and regulations, reflecting the relative strength of special education reform groups. Furthermore, unlike Model Cities, which offered funds to be distributed to a limited number of localities, federal special education reform legislation and Chapter 766 require altered practices in *all* legislative districts. The kind of bargaining for a share of limited divisible resources that was the undoing of Model Cities was not applicable to PL 94–142 or Chapter 766.

31
Wilken and Porter, "State Aid For Special Education," p. III-21. In public hearings some school officials condemned the regulations as too detailed. One called the regulations "the most unbelievable bureaucratic red tape" ("Springfield Officials Blast Chapter 766," *Boston Globe*, March 6, 1976); and another termed the act and regulations a "well-intentioned monstrosity . . . overly advocative" which denied administrators and teachers a substantive role ("Special Education Act Bothers Professionals," *Boston Globe*, March 8, 1974).

32
The initial version of the bill required implementation to begin in September 1973. The Senate Ways and Means Committee, responding to concerns of local school officials, postponed the beginning to September 1974 (Creighton, "Chapter 766," p. 22).

As Jeffrey Pressman has observed, a money-moving mentality, such as characterized many social programs of the 1960s, can lead to a crisis atmosphere in implementation, whereby programs are fielded hastily with the hope that quick results will lend support for the following year's funding. Under such circumstances planning is easily turned into rationalizing actions already taken. See his "Foreign Aid and Urban Aid," in *Neighborhood Control in the 1970s*, ed. George Frederickson (New York: Chandler Publishing Co., 1973).

33
Wilken and Porter, "State Aid for Public Education," pp. 16, 18.

34
State departments of education and their changing roles are considered by K. Fred Daniel and Joseph W. Crenshaw, "What Has Been and Should Be the Role of State Education Agencies in the Development and Implementation of Teacher Education Programs (Both Pre- and Inservice)? A Review and Analysis of Literature," U.S. Office of Education, Order No. OEC-0-71-3315, September 3, 1971.

For an analysis of state department implementation constraints, see Jerome Murphy, *State Education Agencies and Discretionary Funds* (Lexington, Mass.: D.C. Heath, 1974); and his "Title I of ESEA: The Politics of Implementing Federal Education Reform," *Harvard Educational Review* 41, (February, 1971): 35–63.

35
"Massachusetts To Fill 29 Special Education Jobs," *Boston Globe*, August 2, 1973.

36
"State office for Children Proposed by Gov. Sargent," *Boston Globe*, February 9, 1972.

37
"Special Education Law in Effect; Surveillance Planned," *Boston Globe*, September 3, 1974. Results of the monitoring efforts were reported in these later articles: "766 Violations Charged in Report," *Christian Science Monitor*, February 19, 1975; and "Ch. 766 Compliance Uneven, Groups Charge," *Boston Globe*, February 19, 1975.

38
Interview with Robert Audette, associate commissioner, Division of Special Education, July 17, 1975.

39
Creighton, "Chapter 766," p. 27.

40
Internal Division of Special Education document, "766 Update," May 1974.

41
Several unsuccessful attempts had previously been made by special edu-

cation administrators to form such an association, but it took the shared anger and frustration brought on by their relations with the Division of Special Education under Chapter 766 to bring them together.

This example seems to fit the model of a "purposive" organization described by Peter Clark and James Q. Wilson ["Incentive Systems: A Theory of Organizations," *Administrative Science Quarterly* 6 (September 1961): 129-166]. Such an organization provides as incentives to members the sharing of protest and reform objectives.

42
Commonwealth of Massachusetts Authorization of Services, "The Development of a Technical Manual for Chapter 766," June 17, 1974. The contract with the Massachusetts Association of School Business Officials (MASBO) was in the amount of $31,040.

43
Interview with a division staff member.

44
Interview with a division staff person who served as a member of the policy group.

45
Daniel and Crenshaw, "The Role of State Education Agencies."

46
This was the strong consensus of a group of school administrators from different parts of the state interviewed at a special education meeting. This view was echoed by a number of others with whom I met in the course of the study. However, school administrators carefully guarded their autonomy, and while they decried the lack of leadership from the state Department of Education in implementing Chapter 766, at the same time they did not necessarily favor an activist department either.

47
"Massachusetts to Fill 29 Special Education Jobs," *Boston Globe*, August 2, 1973. See also Chapter 766 of the Acts of 1972, Commonwealth of Massachusetts (henceforth referred to as Chapter 766), Section 2, for a description of the powers and duties of the Division of Special Education.

48
Interview with Robert Audette, associate commissioner, Division of Special Education, July 17, 1975. Dr. Audette said that he had been out of school only two years when he joined the division in October 1973 and was consequently lacking administrative experience. (He had held a position at the Fernald State School, a Massachusetts institution for the developmentally disabled, immediately before joining the division.) He said he had hired people from Fernald and other institutions because he had had a poor relationship with the previous associate commissioner, Joseph Rice,

and did not know whom he could trust in the division after Rice's departure.

49
David M. Sheehan, "The Children's Puzzle: A Study of Services to Children in Massachusetts," Report to the House Ways and Means Committee, Institute for Governmental Services, University of Massachusetts, Boston, February 1977, p. 9.

50
Ibid.

51
"Bill to Phase in 766 May Face Court Test," *Boston Globe*, May 9, 1974.

52
Bartley explained his withdrawal of the amendment as necessary to avert a suit. He said, "Federal courts have said this is not a privilege—education for all children is a constitutional right" (Bartley Halts Special Education Debate," *Boston Globe*, May 23, 1974). He may have been referring to the fact that a New Mexico district court just one month earlier had declared a gradual approach unacceptable (Creighton, "Chapter 766," p. 34).

53
Chapter 766, Section 11, s. 13; Section 21.

54
"Unfunded Chapter 766: Who Finally, Will Foot the Bill?" *Boston Globe*, February 24, 1974; and "State Says Extra Ch. 766 Cost Is $40 m., Not $100 m.," Ibid., February 27, 1974.

55
Commonwealth of Massachusetts, House No. 6429, "Second Interim Report of the Special Commission Relative to the Laws of the Commonwealth Pertaining to Elementary and Secondary Education as They Relate to Unequal Educational Opportunity and Services," August 10, 1977, p. 34.

56
"26 M in State Budget to Educate Handicapped Children," *Boston Herald American*, April 9, 1974.

57
"Paying School Costs," *Boston Globe*, March 5, 1974.

58
"Unfunded Chapter 766," *Boston Globe*, February 24, 1974.

59
Interview with David Anderson, May 12, 1978. The chaotic management practices of the state Department of Education, particularly with regard to fiscal matters, are described in fascinating detail by Anderson in *"Mathematical Models and Decision Making in Bureaucracies: A Case Story Told*

from Three Points of View" (Ph.D. diss., Alfred P. Sloan School of Management, Massachusetts Institute of Technology, 1977).

For a detailed account of how the wealthier districts did better than the poorer ones in securing higher levels of state reimbursement, see Wilken and Porter, "State Aid for Public Education," pp. III-28–III-32.

60
Interview with Lawrence Kotin.

61
Commonwealth of Massachusetts, House No. 6429, "Second Interim Report Pertaining to Unequal Educational Opportunity," p. 39.

Chapter 3

1
Commonwealth of Massachusetts, Department of Education, "Regulations for the Implementation of Chapter 766 of the Acts of 1972: The Comprehensive Special Education Law," May 28, 1974 (henceforth referred to as "Regulations"), par. 314.0, p. 17.

2
Ibid., pars. 317.0–317.9, pp. 19–20.

3
Ibid., par. 320.0, pp. 21–22. An intermediate core evaluation may be given, with the parents' approval, in those cases in which it is expected that the child will *not* be placed outside a regular class more than 25 percent of the time. It differs from the full core evaluation only in that a lesser number of assessments are required.

4
Ibid., par. 322.0, p. 23.

5
David M. Sheehan, "The Children's Puzzle," Report to the Massachusetts House Ways and Means Committee, Institute for Governmental Services, University of Massachusetts, Boston, Mass., February 1977, p. 5.

6
William H. Wilken and David O. Porter, "State Aid for Special Education: Who Benefits?" The National Foundation for the Improvement of Education and the National Conference of State Legislatures, Washington, D.C., May 31, 1976, p. III-16.

7
Based on the "Claim for State Aid to Special Education Programs," form SPED 5, for the years ending June 30, 1973, and June 30, 1974.

8
Wilken and Porter, "State Aid for Special Education," p. III-29.

9
Ibid., p. III–32.

10
Sheehan, "The Children's Puzzle," pp. 6, 7.

11
A school board member from another town said that his community had profited greatly from the services of a fiscal consultant who specialized in helping school systems find ways to maximize their reimbursements from the state.

12
An additional factor inhibiting cooperation and collaboration among school systems in program development was their competition with one another for limited federal grant funds administered by the state Department of Education. As a result, at least some school administrators believed that a sharing of ideas might be at the expense of their system's competitive advantage in securing federal discretionary grants through the state Department of Education. Chapter 766 provided incentives for local systems to cooperate in establishing educational "collaboratives," and a number of school systems have joined together in these kinds of arrangements. This development is discussed in William H. Wilken and John J. Callahan, "Disparities in Special Education Services: The Need for Better Fiscal Management," Legislators' Action Project, National Conference of State Legislatures, Washington, D.C., August 31, 1976, pp. 44–45.

13
"Regulations," par. 311.0, p. 15. Emphasis added.

Chapter 4

1
Of forty meetings in which I participated, thirteen were in system A, eleven in system B, and sixteen in system C. This represents 13.5, 2.6, and 6.5 percent respectively of the total number of evaluations completed by each of the three school systems during this six-month period. While a random selection of evaluation meetings was not possible, in systems B and C I was free to attend whatever meetings were scheduled on the days that I was present. Permission of parents was obtained beforehand. There were two instances in system C where school personnel asked that I not attend because serious conflict with the parents over the team's recommendation was anticipated, and they feared an appeal. Aside from these two cases, there is every reason to believe that the evaluation meetings observed were typical of those being conducted in systems B and C during this period.

Administrative personnel in system A were somewhat more guarded; there I was excluded from perhaps as many as five or six meetings that were considered "sensitive." Furthermore, there was no direct access to evaluations conducted in the schools by school-based teams, although I did observe two meetings held on a day when I was in one of the schools interviewing. It is likely therefore that the sample of evaluations observed in system A was skewed toward what school personnel judged to be "routine."

Of the forty meetings observed, twenty-five different schools were represented. Twenty-five of the meetings concerned males and fifteen females. The ages of the children ranged from four to eighteen, with a mean age of ten, and their grade placement from preschool through grade twelve, the mean being grade five. The sample closely resembled the total population of children evaluated in these respects.

2

For a discussion of the function of status-conferring ceremonies in organizations processing people on a mass basis, see Stanton Wheeler, "The Structure of Formally Organized Socialization Settings," in Orville G. Brim, Jr., and Stanton Wheeler, Socialization after Childhood: Two Essays (New York: John Wiley and Sons, 1966), pp. 53–116.

3

Names and, where necessary, circumstances have been slightly altered to prevent identification of those involved or discussed in these meetings. Otherwise these accounts accurately reflect what took place.

4

Murray Edelman has called attention to the use of technical language by professionals to assert dominance over clients. See "The Political Language of the Helping Professions," in Political Language: Words That Succeed and Policies That Fail (New York: Academic Press, 1977), ch. 4, pp. 57–75; also in Politics and Society 4 (Fall 1974): 295–310.

The relative ranking of professional groups in health and welfare organizations is discussed by Robert D. Vinter, "Analysis of Treatment Organizations," in Human Services Organizations, ed. Yeheskel Hasenfeld and Richard A. English (Ann Arbor, Mich.: University of Michigan Press, 1974), pp. 35–50, esp. 42–44. See also Eliot Freidson, Professional Dominance: The Social Structure of Medical Care (New York: Atherton Press, 1970), esp. ch. 5, pp. 127–164.

5

"The results of standardized or local tests of ability, aptitude, affect, achievement or aspiration or projective personality tests shall not be used exclusively or principally as the basis for any finding or conclusion" [Commonwealth of Massachusetts, Department of Education, "Regulations for the Implementation of Chapter 766 of the Acts of 1972: The Comprehensive Special Education Law," May 28, 1974, par. 209.0, p. 7 (henceforth referred to as "Regulations")].

The regulations for PL 94–142 also prohibit exclusive reliance on test

scores: "In interpreting evaluation data and in making placement decisions, each public agency shall: (1) Draw upon information from a
variety of sources, including aptitude and achievement tests, teacher recommendations, physical condition, social or cultural background, and
adaptive behavior" ("Rules and Regulations," Department of Health, Education, and Welfare, Office of Education, Education of Handicapped Children, Implementation of Part B of the Education of the Handicapped
Act, *Federal Register* 42:163, August 23, 1977, par. 121a.533(a), p. 42497).

6
Maryann K. Hoff et al., "Notice and Consent: The School's Responsibility to
Inform Parents," *Journal of School Psychology*, forthcoming, abstract, pp.
11, 12. (Page references are from the original manuscript.)

7
Ibid., p. 11.

8
Reported in "Summary of Research Findings on Individualized Education
Programs," National Association of State Directors of Special Education,
Washington, D.C., 1978, pp. 3–4.

9
Ibid., p. 8.

10
A comparative analysis of the literacy levels of welfare clients and the
language employed in the application materials they must complete offers
another example of bureaucracy's failure to communicate with clients. The
study showed that the written materials used by welfare offices are generally at a level well beyond what most potential clients can comprehend.
The authors conclude that the mismatch between client reading skills and
welfare agency procedures and documents contributes to high error rates
and bars the enrollment of clients for public welfare benefits. This literacy
barrier is consistent with the unofficial policies of many public welfare
agencies to restrict access to public assistance and social services. See Marc
Bendick, Jr., and Mario G. Cantu, "The Literacy of Welfare Clients," *Social
Service Review* 52 (March 1978): 56–68.

11
"Regulations," par. 207.0, p. 6; *Federal Register* 42:163, August 23, 1977, par.
121a334, (a)(5), p. 42490.

12
Alan M. Orenstein, "Chapter 766: The Massachusetts Special Needs Law"
(A research report for the CECD/CERI meeting on Education and the Integration of Community Services, Cambridge, Mass., August 15, 1976), mimeographed, pp. 40–41.

13

National School Public Relations Assocation, *Educating All the Handi-capped* (Arlington, Va.: 1977), p. 31. The outcome of the Supreme Court appeal had not yet been decided at the time this was being written.

14

Appeals procedures are required of the states under PL 94-142, *Federal Register* 42:163, August 23, 1977, pars. 121a.506-121a.514, pp. 42495-42496. In Massachusetts the parent has forty-five days after the assessment meeting in which to give written acceptance of the education plan ["Regulations," par. 325.8 (a)]. At the expiration of that waiting period, the parent may reject the provisions of the plan and appeal the school's decision to the Bureau of Child Advocacy of the Division of Special Education, with or without a hearing. Further appeals are possible, ending with adjudication by the Superior Court ("Regulations," ch. 4, "Appeal Procedures," pars. 400.0-410.0, pp. 40-45).

As of June 9, 1975, the Bureau of Child Advocacy had had 234 cases come before it. The bureau director stated that of those completed, decisions were "running two to one in favor of the schools."

The differential utilization of the appeals process by rich and poor parents was illustrated by the fact that most appeals were coming from affluent Boston suburban communities and most involved disputes about payment for expensive private school placements. Boston schools, with the largest enrollment in the state and a past record of widespread violation of special education statutes, had had only one appeal. (Interview with Keith Rawlings, director, Bureau of Child Advocacy.) See also Milton Budoff, Sibyl Mitchell, and Lawrence Kotin, "Procedural Due Process: Its Application to Special Education and Its Implications for Teacher Training" (Cambridge, Mass.: Research Institute for Educational Problems, August 1976).

In response to concerns of school officials that they could be held legally accountable for meeting the goals set forth in the IEP, the final draft of the regulations for PL 94-142 specifies that "Part B of the Act does not require that any agency, teacher, or other person be held accountable if a child does not achieve the growth projected in the annual goals and objectives." *Federal Register* 42:163, August 23, 1977, par. 121a.349, p. 42491.

15

Orenstein, "Chapter 766," p. 42.

16

"Regulations," par. 318.0, p. 20.

17

Ibid., par. 311.0, pp. 15-16; par. 317.5, p. 19.

18

Ibid., par. 208.0. pp. 6-7

19

In recognition of this problem, PL 94–142 regulations provide that IEP meetings may be conducted without a parent in attendance if the school cannot convince the parent to attend. The school must, however, document its attempts to arrange for the parents' attendance through records of telephone calls, letters, and home visits (*Federal Register* 42:163, August 23, 1977, par. 121a.345, pp. 42490–42491).

20

Stephen J. Apter, "Applications of Ecological Theory: Toward a Community Special Education Model," *Exceptional Children* 43 (March 1977): 366–373; also Nicholas Hobbs, *The Futures of Children* (San Francisco: Jossey-Bass, 1975). For an earlier statement on the limitations of a medical model approach that endeavors to fit the child to the school, see Charles Silberman, *Crisis in the Classroom* (New York: Random House, 1970).

21

William Ryan, *Blaming the Victim* (New York: Vintage Books, 1971).

22

Erving Goffman has noted the tendency of institutional personnel to interpret all statements and activities of inmates as confirming the official diagnosis of them. He terms such behavior "the automatic identification of the inmate." See *Asylums* (Garden City, New York: Anchor Books, 1961). For an example of how mental hospital staff interpret the normal behavior of inmates as "psychotic," see D. L. Rosenau, "On Being Sane in Insane Places," *Science* 179 (June 1973): 250–258.

23

Howard S. Becker discusses ways in which teachers secure their work environment against intrusion from parents in "The Teacher in the Authority System of the Public School," in *Human Service Organizations*, ed. Hasenfeld and English, pp. 378–391.

Chapter 5

1

In his *Crisis in the Classroom* (New York: Random House, 1970), Charles Silberman characterizes the education literature as overly preoccupied with analyzing why children fail, rather than considering why schools fail. He notes that the prevailing tendency is to shape the child to fit the school rather than the school program to the child (see esp. pp. 79–95). Why this is the case is suggested by Erving Goffman. The subordination of client needs to both latent and manifest organization practices employed to expedite the mass processing of clients is a central theme of *Asylums* (Garden City, New York: Doubleday, 1961). While schools are not total institutions, many of the same forces shaping client-staff relations are at work in both. See also Stanton Wheeler, "The Structure of Formally Organized Socialization Settings," in Orville G. Brim and Stanton Wheeler, *Socialization after Childhood: Two Essays*, (New York: John Wiley and Sons, 1966).

2
Chapter 766, Section 1.

3
No one could explain the reason for continuing to segregate boys and girls in separate special education classes except to state that the practice had traditionally been followed in this school system. As one teacher put it, "I don't know. It's just the way we've always done it here."

4
David L. Kirp assesses the implication of slotting practices (although he does not use that term) in "Schools as Sorters: The Constitutional and Policy Implications of Student Classification," *University of Pennsylvania Law Review* 121 (April 1973): 705–797.

5
The term "superordinate" is used by Robert D. Vinter to describe the dominant ranking of certain professions within health and welfare organizations. See "Analysis of Treatment Organizations," in *Human Service Organizations*, eds. Yeheskel Hasenfeld and Richard A. English, pp. 33–50, esp. 43–44.

6
"Regulations (k)," pp. 60–61.

7
The pressuring of parents to accept retention in grade or nonpromotion of a child is *not* typical, but unfortunately neither is it uncommon. By way of contrast, consider this example from a different school in the same system. A mother questions the promotion of her child into the third grade. The principal reassures the mother saying, "I have no reservations. We are going to meet her needs in the third grade no matter what level she is reading at."

Chapter 6

1
For example, in the three school systems studied, 128 children of a total combined enrollment of 26,683 were reported to be in "substantially separate" programs as of June 1974.

2
The need for and implications of teacher autonomy are discussed by Charles E. Bidwell in "The School as a Formal Organization," in *Handbook of Organizations*, ed. James G. March (Chicago: Rand McNally, 1965), pp. 972–1022.

3
"Regulations," par. 316.1, p. 18; par. 320.2, p. 21; par. 323.1 (c), p. 24; and pars. 323.2 and 323.3, p. 25.

4

See also Bidwell, "The School as a Formal Organization."

5

These are among benefiits listed in the Foundation for Exceptional Children's publication, *A Primer on Individualized Education Programs for Handicapped Children* as cited in *Educating All the Handicapped* (Arlington, Va.: National School Public Relations Association, 1977), p. 58.

6

National Association of State Directors of Special Education, "Summary of Research Findings on Individualized Education Programs" (Washington, D.C., 1978), p. 8.

7

The evidence suggests that nationwide such disparities are more the rule than the exception and are associated with local and regional differences in wealth, leadership, and parent advocacy group pressure, as well as shifting definitions of specific handicapping conditions. See William H. Wilken and John J. Callahan, "Disparities in Special Education Services: The Need for Better Fiscal Management," Legislators Education Action Project, National Conference of State Legislatures, Washington, D.C., August 31, 1976; and James S. Kakalik, "Policy Issues in Cost and Finance of Special Education," WN-9680-HEW mimeo (Santa Monica, Calif.: Rand Corporation, 1977).

8

"Regulations," par. 322.4, p. 23; par. 338.1 (a), p. 38.

9

For purposes of analysis, I have grouped together all children and all teachers, since the size of the sample precluded separate analysis by school or even school system. One expects to find some differences in teacher responses reflecting differences in the populations served and policies pursued by individual schools. The failure to consider such differences here reflects the limits of the methodology employed rather than a belief that such differences were unimportant.

10

"Regulations," par. 322.0, pp. 23–24.

11

Commonwealth of Massachusetts, House No. 6429, "Second Interim Report Pertaining to Elementary and Secondary Education as They Relate to Unequal Educational Opportunity and Services," August 10, 1977.

12

"Summary of Research Findings on Individualized Education Programs," p. 1.

13

The legislature's special commission on Chapter 766 reported that "some resource rooms are used as 'dumping grounds' . . . and detention centers, . . . [and] some [children] are there without education plans." Commonwealth of Massachusetts, House No. 6429, "Second Interim Report," p. 32.

14
These categories were hearing, vision, mobility, speech, or learning disorder, behavioral development, family counseling, and other. While this choice of categories leaves much to be desired, they were used for the sake of consistency in coding teacher responses. These same categories are used by all school systems throughout the state to indicate reasons for referring a child for evaluation. The required use of such vague categories was symptomatic of the lack of sophistication about management information systems in the Division of Special Education.

15
The individual education plan forms, from which the statistics shown in table 7 were compiled, indicate services recommended; however, this does not necessarily mean that the child has received these services. There was usually a long delay between the completion of the education plan and its implementation.

16
Thomas J. Kelley et al., "Behavioral Disorders: Teachers' Perceptions," *Exceptional Children* 43 (February 1977): 316–318.

17
William H. Wilken and David O. Porter, "State Aid for Special Education: Who Benefits?" National Foundation for the Improvement of Education and the National Conference of State Legislatures, Washington, D.C., May 31, 1976, table I–7.

18
U.S. Department of Health, Education, and Welfare, Bureau of Education for the Handicapped, "BEH Data Notes," September 1977.

19
This 0.6 percent figure is derived by dividing Wilken and Porter's estimate of the total public school enrollment for 1972 (45, 905, 244) into the 1977 BEH estimate of 284,385 children receiving services for "emotional disturbance." See Wilken and Porter, table 1–7, and "BEH Data Notes," September 1977.

20
John Junkala, "Teachers' Assessments and Team Decisions," *Exceptional Children* 44 (September 1977): 31, 32.

21
A study by SRI International of 150 IEPs in fifteen school districts in three states found that while teachers usually made the referrals in rural districts, other school personnel along with teachers made the referrals in the urban

districts ("Summary of Research Findings on Individualized Education Programs," p. 3).

22

This was also found to be true in other Massachusetts school districts. One observer reports, "Bridgeport's systemwide team performed over 325 evaluations during the first year, a remarkable feat of assembly-line evaluating. Variables such as the disruptiveness of the child's classroom behavior and the clamor that his parents raised in demanding services determined priorities." [Alan M. Orenstein, "Chapter 766: The Massachusetts Special Needs Law" (A research report for the CECD/CERI meeting on Education and the Integration of Community Services, Cambridge, Mass., August 15, 1976), mimeographed, p. 71.]

23

"Regulations," par. 338.1, p. 38. The requirement of written progress reports was, as far as I could determine universally ignored during the first year of Chapter 766 implementation.

24

I do not wish to imply through the generic use of the term "specialist" that all specialists are equal. To the contrary, my observations of core evaluation meetings revealed a definite status hierarchy among specialists, with those whose crafts involved the use of IQ and other standardized tests at the top. Teachers, together with parents, were definitely at the bottom.

25

Commonwealth of Massachusetts, House No. 6429, "Second Interim Report of the Special Commission," p. 33.

26

This was found to be true in the SRI International study of IEPs as summarized in the "Summary of Research Findings on Individualized Education Programs," National Association of State Directors of Special Education, p. 3, as well as in my review of education plans in three Massachusetts school districts.

27

The Massachusetts Legislature's Special Commission on Chapter 766 reported, "Many regular education teachers . . . seem to have very little understanding of the law or regulations . . . [and] do not know how to identify, refer, or meet the needs of special needs students" ("Second Interim Report of the Special Commission," p. 32).

28

Maynard C. Reynolds, "More Process Than Is Due," *Theory into Practice* 14 (April 1975): 67–68.

29

The Massachusetts regulations provide that no more than four children with special needs may be placed in one regular classroom without specific written permission from the Regional Office of the Division of Special Education (par. 502.10, p. 58). No distinction, however, is made regarding the nature or severity of the child's condition, thus rendering this provision meaningless.

According to the local president of the Massachusetts Teachers Association for system B, that local was seeking a union contract provision to relieve the classroom teacher of two "regular" children for each special needs child assigned to his or her class. That this is also a national concern of teachers is suggested in an article by Fred M. Hechinger, "Bringing the Handicapped into the Mainstream," New York Times, April 26, 1976, p. ES-15. Hechinger describes union views nationally as follows: "Teachers' unions and organizations are somewhat ambivalent about the new approach. But there are strong indications that future contracts will aim at protecting the growing army of special teachers for the handicapped while insisting that for every mainstreamed handicapped child the class size be reduced by three children."

Chapter 7

1
Martin J. Kaufman et al., "Mainstreaming: Toward an Explication of the Concept," Focus on Exceptional Children 7 (May 1975): 1-12.

2
Chapter 766, Section 11, s. 2.

3
U.S. Department of Health, Education, and Welfare, Office of Education, "Education of Handicapped Children, Rules and Regulations," Federal Register 42:163, August 23, 1977, par. 121a.550, p. 42497.

4
These data are from the districts' year-end reports to the state. From 1973 to 1974 there was a slight shift in these districts of children from separate classes to partially integrated classes, but this shift represented an increased integration of special class children for a portion of the school day—for physical education, art, and music, for example—rather than a return of special class children to regular classes.

5
"Regulations," par. 336.0, p. 37.

6
"Chapter 766—New Hopes and New Fears," Boston Globe, March 17, 1974; and "Special Ed Law Upsets Some Parents," Boston Globe, June 6, 1974.

7
Commonwealth of Massachusetts, House No. 6429, "Second Interim Re-

port of the Special Commission Relative to the Laws of the Commonwealth Pertaining to Elementary and Secondary Education as They Relate to Unequal Educational Opportunity and Services," August 10, 1977, p. 14.

8

William H. Wilken and John J. Callahan, "Disparities in Special Education Services: The Need for Better Fiscal Management," Legislators' Education Action Project, National Conference of State Legislatures, Washington, D.C., August 31, 1976, p. 36.

9

Commonwealth of Massachusetts, House No. 6429, "Second Interim Report of the Special Commission," p. 32.

10

Ibid., pp. 43–44.

11

"Regulations on Special Education to Hike Taxes," Boston Globe, February 22, 1974; and "Questions, Answers on Chapter 766 Special Education Law," Boston Globe, August 25, 1974. These estimates were derived by applying the widely accepted national incidence figures of 12 percent to the state's school population.

In the absence of a comprehensive national epidemiological survey of the incidence of various handicapping conditions in the general population, the overall 12 percent figure and other estimates of specific conditions should be regarded as nothing more than convenient points of reference. Unfortunately the continued use of such estimates of incidence by the U.S. Bureau of Education for the Handicapped lends them a ring of truth unjustified by their derivation.

12

"Regulations," pars. 300.0–308.0, pp. 9–13.

13

John Junkala, "Teachers' Assessments and Team Decisions," Exceptional Children 44 (September 1977): 32.

14

"Regulations," par. 317.0, p. 19; and pars. 325.8 (a) and 326.0, p. 31.

15

In the three systems studied the time required to complete an evaluation was determined for each child by calculating the number of days from the date of referral to the date of the "parent conference" as shown on education plan forms. (The "parent conference" was actually the evaluation team meeting and, under Massachusetts regulations, should have been held within thirty-five days after referral.)

16
The mean and median time required (in months) to complete evaluations and the standard deviation in the three systems were as follows:

	Mean	Median	Standard Deviation
System A	6.92	4.50	6.90
System B	7.78	6.98	4.13
System C	7.94	6.98	5.11

For system B, which had a better record-keeping system, these findings were based on the 85.1 percent of the cases for which complete data on referral and completion dates were available; for system C, comparable data were available for only 59.7 percent of the children for whom evaluations had been completed; and for system A, only 16.7 percent. As these data suggest, the record keeping varied from adequate to abysmal. System B, which took what might be termed a more bureaucratic approach to implementation, had hired a consultant to establish a record-keeping work-flow and monitoring system. It also hired more new staff than the other systems and referred and evaluated relatively more children, but in a much more routine and cursory way. The other two systems developed their own record-keeping procedures internally with less favorable results. There was virtually no guidance in this crucial implementation component from the Division of Special Education.

17
At the end of June 1975, system A, had completed 228 cases and had 60 known "pending" cases plus an undetermined number of incomplete evaluations started by individual schools. System C, with 330 completed, had 192 incomplete, many of which were May and June referrals.

18
Chapter 766, Section 1.

19
See James Q. Wilson, "The Bureaucracy Problem," *The Public Interest* 6 (Winter 1967): 3–9.

20
"Rules and Regulations," *Federal Register* 42:163, August 23, 1977, par. 121a.320, p. 42489.

21
One local observer estimates that there has been close to a 50 percent turnover of directors of special education in Massachusetts between 1974 and 1978, reflecting the increased stress on them since the start of Chapter 766 (interview with Milton Budoff, February 1, 1978).

22

In system B, 66.2 percent of parent referrals, as compared with 56.4 percent of teacher referrals, were completed in less than eight months. (Principal referrals accounted for a negligible percentage of all referrals.) In system C 73.7 percent of parent referrals and 78.5 percent of principal referrals were completed in less than eight months, while only 53.8 percent of teacher referrals were.

These data tend to confirm the proposition developed in observing many client-processing bureaucracies: clients who complain tend to be accommodated, although agencies discourage complaints in a variety of ways. Since I could not control for the severity of need represented by different referral sources, the possibility exists that parent referrals were processed more quickly because the cases they referred presented greater need than referrals of teachers. I do not believe this to be true, however. I was told again and again that parent demand was among the most salient determinants of institutional response.

23

Wilken and Porter, "State Aid for Special Education," p. III-38.

24

In all three school systems, consistent with national patterns, boys outnumbered girls two or three to one in their presence in special education programs.

25

Male teachers are reportedly more tolerant of disruptive behavior than females. See Thomas J. Kelley et al., "Behavioral Disorders: Teachers' Perceptions," *Exceptional Children* 43 (February 1977): 316-318.

26

U.S. Department of Health, Education, and Welfare, Bureau of Education for the Handicapped, "BEH Data Notes" (Washington, D.C., September 1977).

27

Wilken and Callahan, "Disparities," p. 3.

28

The deference of laymen to professionals and of certain categories of professionals to others is discussed by Eliot Freidson in *Professional Dominance: The Social Structure of Medical Care* (New York: Atherton Press, 1970), esp. ch. 5, pp. 127-164. See also Robert D. Vinter, "Analysis of Treatment Organizations," in *Human Service Organizations*, ed. Yeheskel Hasenfeld and Richard A. English (Ann Arbor, Mich.: University of Michigan Press, 1974), pp. 33-50, esp. pp. 42-44 for a discussion of what he terms the "superordination of professions" in direct service health and welfare agencies.

29
Chapter 766, Section 11, s. 2.

30
Interview with Robert Audette.

31
"Ch. 766 Changes Opposed at Hearing," *Boston Globe*, June 17, 1975.

32
Report of Newton von Sander, Wellesley, "Summary of A.S.E. Spring Conference, June 6, Sturbridge" (dated June 11, 1975), p. 5. These complaints were prominent among testimony presented at a June 27, 1975, meeting on Chapter 766, cosponsored by the governor and the Massachusetts Association of School Superintendents.

33
Massachusetts Rehabilitation Commission, Clients Services Memorandum No. 42, "Chapter 766 Policy," from Commissioner O'Connell to Professional Staff, May 23, 1975, p. 1. The commissioner justified this action on the grounds that federal regulations prohibited the expenditure of federal rehabilitation funds for persons eligible for state-financed services.

34
Commonwealth of Massachusetts, House No. 6429, "Second Interim Report of the Special Commission," p. 25.

35
Alan M. Orenstein, "Chapter 766: The Massachusetts Special Needs Law" (A research report for the CECD/CERI meeting on Education and the Integration of Community Services, Cambridge, Mass., August 15, 1976), p. 5.

36
Commonwealth of Massachusetts, House No. 6429, "Second Interim Report of the Special Commission," p. 29.

37
David M. Sheehan, "The Children's Puzzle: A Study of Services to Children in Massachusetts," Institute for Governmental Services, University of Massachusetts, Boston, Mass., February 1977, p. 10.

38
Wilken and Callahan, "Disparities," p. 42.

39
Commonwealth of Massachusetts, House No. 6429, "Second Interim Report of the Special Commission," p. 27.

40
"Rules and Regulations," *Federal Register* 42:163, August 23, 1977, p. 42501.

41
Wilken and Porter, "State Aid for Special Education," p. I-4.

42
Ibid., p. 37. For an assessment of alternative models of state coordination of services to handicapped children, see Wilken and Callahan, "Disparities," pp. 23–29, 42–44.

43
"Second Interim Report of the Special Commission," p. 43.

44
Chapter 766, Section 11, s. 2.

45
Ibid.

46
Interview with Robert Crabtree, former research director, Massachusetts Joint Committee on Education.

47
Commonwealth of Massachusetts, Department of Education, Division of Special Education, form SPED 5, "Claim for State Aid to Special Education Programs" (revised May 1973).

48
"Rules and Regulations," *Federal Register* 42:163, August 23, 1977, pars. 121a380–121a387, pp. 42492–42493.

49
National School Public Relations Association, *Educating All the Handicapped* (Arlington, Va.: 1977), p. 78. The quote is from a September 1976 report of the General Accounting Office which criticizes the current BEH training emphasis.

50
Gweneth B. Brown and Douglas J. Palmer, "A Review of BEH Funded Personnel Preparation Programs in Emotional Disturbance," *Exceptional Children* 44 (November 1977): 168–174.

Wilken and Porter argue that the debate over a specialist or generalist emphasis is more a political than strictly educational issue:

Those who argue for the competency of the generalist teacher tend to have strong ties to schools of education and their liberal arts traditions. Those who argue for the specialist teacher often have much closer ties to medical schools and the hard sciences. Indeed, one of the keys to understanding the division of opinion is to recognize that what is at issue is not simply the merits of generalist teachers relative to specialist teachers, but the closely related question of who is to control institutions which train special education teachers.

(Wilken and Porter, "State Aid for Special Education," p. II-30).

Chapter 8

1

Recent works in this vein include Samuel Bowles and Herbert Gintis, *Schooling in Capitalist America* (New York: Basic Books, 1976); Colin Greer, *The Great School Legend* (New York: Viking Press, 1973); Michael Katz, *Class, Bureaucracy, and the Schools* (New York: Praeger Publishers, 1971); Martin Carnoy and Henry M. Levin, eds., *The Limits of Education Reform* (New York: David McKay Co., 1976); and Miriam Wasserman, *The School Fix* (New York: Outerbridge and Dienstfrey, 1970).

2

Carnoy and Levin, *Limits*, pp. 9–10.

3

Upon his resignation as associate commissioner of the Massachusetts Department of Education, Robert Audette expressed concern that "we're not doing a good job with high school programs and young kids getting in trouble with the law. They end up with the Department of Youth Services. If they're well-to-do, they become special–needs students. But if they're poor and minorities, they end up being viewed as criminals. They have no advocates." *Boston Globe*, Monday, May 30, 1977, p. 31.

4

Michael W. Kirst, review of Mike M. Milstein, *Impact and Response: Federal Aid and State Education Agencies* (New York: Teachers College Press, Columbia University, 1976) in *Policy Analysis* 4 (Spring 1978): 282–284.

5

See, in addition to the Milstein book reviewed by Kirst, Jerome T. Murphy, *State Education Agencies and Discretionary Funds* (Lexington, Mass.: Lexington Books, 1974); and David O. Porter et al., *The Politics of Budgeting Federal Aid: Resource Mobilization by Local School Districts* (Beverly Hill, Calif.: Sage Professional Paper in Administration and Policy Studies, 03–003, 1973).

6

This is the term employed by Erving Goffman to describe the informal adjustments of institutional staff members. See *Asylums* (New York: Doubleday, 1961).

7

Murray Edelman has pointed out the inherent limitations of addressing what are essentially political problems with administrative solutions. See *Political Language: Words That Succeed and Policies That Fail* (New York: Academic Press, 1977).

8

Robert D. Vinter, "Analysis of Treatment Organizations," in *Human Service*

Organizations, eds. Yeheskel Hasenfeld and Richard A. English (Ann Arbor, Mich.: University of Michigan Press, 1974), pp. 33–50.

9

For an elaboration of this view, see Frances Fox Piven and Richard A. Cloward, *Regulating the Poor: The Functions of Public Welfare* (New York: Pantheon Books, 1971) and Jeffrey Galper, *The Politics of Social Services* (Englewood Cliffs, N.J.: Prentice-Hall, 1975).

10

The symbolic function of legislation to provide reassurance to publics has been discussed by Murray Edelman. See *Politics as Symbolic Action: Mass Arousal and Quiescence* (New York: Academic Press, 1971).

11

The relationship between the state of the economy and the identification of what are deemed to be social problems has been analyzed by S. M. Miller, "The Political Economy of Social Problems: From the Sixties to the Seventies," *Social Problems* 24 (October 1976): 131–141.

Index